# IS GOD ANGRY?

## *A Perspective Through Moses*

Tony Cross

ISBN 978-1-0980-7014-4 (paperback)
ISBN 978-1-0980-7015-1 (digital)

Christian Faith Publishing, Inc.
832 Park Avenue
Meadville, PA 16335
www.christianfaithpublishing.com

Printed in the United States of America

# PREFACE

TRUTH. SPEAKING TO JESUS, PILATE'S famous words were "What is truth?" An interesting question to ask Jesus, who also proclaimed, "I Am the way, the truth, and the life." My dad, whom I love very much, taught me many good things regarding faith, godly living, patience, humility, long-suffering, fatherhood, parenting, etc. But he also said things like "A wino, who drinks wine till he's drunk every day, can drink a glass of water the next day and get drunk all over again." I had no reason to doubt him as a child, because I didn't drink and had no knowledge of the subject of alcohol or alcohol abuse or its effect on the physical body. Google didn't exist. The only computers that existed were at NASA, so researching information was limited and sketchy. It fit his narrative as a pastor, which was to scare everyone into salvation and away from the evils of society. But it wasn't true.

My dad didn't intentionally mislead. He didn't drink. He probably heard it from somewhere, but he did decide to use it without verifying its accuracy. He gave credibility to the source from which he heard it. As I discovered this deception, my belief in my dad as a purveyor of truth began to crumble. What else did he teach me that wasn't true? Drinking and dancing was a sin! Again, not true. As I grew and began looking at the world around me, I was exposed to all kinds of beliefs that were very different from the ones programmed into me as a child. I started a quest to discover for myself what I believed. I also wanted to know why I believed it and be able to support my reason for believing it. Supporting answers like "Just because," or "It's what I was taught," or "Because there was this friend of a friend that was this super-respected theologian that existed before Noah's ark and witnessed it all," weren't good enough.

Subtle deception. If you believe in Satan, he works in this space very effectively. If what we have always believed to be true turned out not to be true, when would you want to know about it? Part of the purpose for this book is to get you to become concerned enough about truth to pour research into what you believe and why. Our entire life's purpose, message, and legacy to future generations depend on its credibility.

This is of paramount importance! Because the subjects that many families are juggling today are very similar, such as "Do we play the Santa Claus game with our children, or the Easter Bunny?" There's no judgment being passed here no matter what you believe or choose to practice with your family. I'm just opening this book using the discussion about truth versus deception—white lies, half-truths, what we've always believed to be true, etc.

We are now living in a culture where the breakdown of the family is leaving a tidal wave of angry, hurting, confused, abused, and violent children. In my experience in counseling with jail inmates, I discovered that almost every inmate had either an extremely corrupt father-child relationship or, more commonly, no relationship at all. As I counseled with them, it became increasingly clear that they had a deep-seated anger. Many of them wanted to change the course of their life. However, they were trapped by their unresolved anger. Some externalized their anger in violence; others internalized it with an extremely self-destructive, low self-esteem, often resulting in drug or alcohol addiction.

The main purpose of this book is to apply truth to determine a discoverable reality of God the Father's true character, rather than what we've always believed it to be. This is a result of my search for truth about who God is, more precisely, who God is as a Father. What is His character and nature really like? Is He an angry God? Why did He command the Israelites to kill everyone in the cities—men, women, children, even the livestock? Taking the life of every "first-born" child and animal in Egypt during the Passover event seemed cruel to me as a child. Who is the Almighty Creator God? How can someone who calls for this kind of action love us? Can we trust a God like this as a Father to us? If you believe that God and Jesus are One

4

and the same, then how can a God who lives toward mankind in this apparent way line up with the patient, kind, loving, gentle, wise Jesus of the New Testament? Why, or why not?

My conclusion is that there is an infallible source of truth that can always be trusted as being eternally unchangeable. It is God Himself! The Creator of it all. The Only One who exists from before everything began. For this book, I start with the assumption that if God were powerful enough to create the world and universe from nothingness with the breath of His spoken Word alone, then He is powerful enough to provide an instruction book about life, for life eternally, and preserve it without flaw throughout all of time, no matter what men may try to do. The Bible, then, becomes the source of truth. The Bible and events written in it for us as a guide for life are not subject to our own interpretation. The written Word is the interpreter of itself. You can choose to disagree with this presumption if you will, but my question to you would be "Then what is your source of truth?" Will it pass the scrutiny of testing its accuracy? My quest on how I concluded I could believe and trust Him and His Word as truth is a different story. Maybe I will live long enough to write about that as well someday.

# Moses—"Prince of Egypt?"

One of the more vivid memories I think of often, are of a church who protested on cultural issues of society from 1990 through as recent as 2015 who were known for carrying signs that read "God Hates Fags" among other things. It deeply troubled me. The ones interviewed seemed angry. The founder argued that it was their sacred duty to warn others of God's anger! How did this behavior line up with "God is love?" There have been more recent protests over several wrongful deaths caused by overzealous police action against black men. The protests, which in some cases may be legitimate over an injustice, followed by looting businesses and setting the town on fire had nothing to do with the injustice. However, in these examples there is a belief system in play.

What causes one person to react violently to an injustice, causing injury, or destruction to another person or person's property, yet someone else treats that same or even a worse injustice with kindness, forgiveness, and on a rare occasion even a love beyond understanding? Why does one teacher build a positive relationship with the student to encourage learning while another uses the hammer of discipline and browbeating? Why would one preacher intensify focus on the message of love, forgiveness, and redemption while another loudly and firmly reiterates a fire and brimstone message on the condemnation of sin?

We have all witnessed, at least from a distance, these conflicting contrasts in human responses. Human beings are extremely complicated. We can't begin to know how or why a culmination of a person's past experiences, personality traits, teachings and beliefs formulate such diverse reactions to life's events. But I have come to believe there is one link that is common to all of us that plays a huge part in this human response mechanism. Perhaps it is the most powerful influence that determines which direction a person takes at this fork in the road on these conditioned responses. It revolves around the persons belief about "Is God Angry?"

The phrase "anger of the LORD" and "anger of the LORD burned against" are used quite frequently throughout the OLD Testament. One interesting note is that the phrase "Anger of the LORD" is not used in the New Testament at all, not even once! Why? As Moses is considered the author of the Pentateuch (the first 5 books of the Old Testament), his writings from his viewpoint would affect much of scripture, including the way the Israelites viewed God the Father.

In this book I want to explore with you how a troubled area of Moses' life affected his view of God, and how this perspective affected his own life and the lives of the Israelite people. But more importantly, we will look at how God the Father dealt with Moses as His true character of love, grace, and compassion was revealed. Subsequently, how his new understanding of God the Father's true character changed Moses' life! The intended purpose of this book is to reveal how Moses' life changed, as his corrupted view of God the Father's character was replaced by God's true character as a Father. My prayer is that our lives would also be changed as we replace our own corrupted view of the Father with the truth of His real character. So that we may experience Him as He is.

As we study Moses' life, keep in mind that the best interpreter of scripture, is scripture itself. Therefore, when we encounter a passage that seems to contradict another passage in scripture, we should then search all other related scriptures to find the silver thread of truth found throughout the Bible as a whole. By this, we will understand

His written word better. By this process, our doctrine and theology will be sound. Let's look at an example:

The passage in **2 Samuel 24:1** tells us that the "anger of the Lord" incited David to take a census of Israel, which was a sin. We know in **James 1:13** Paul said that "God cannot be tempted by evil, and He *(God)* does not tempt anyone." This thread of scripture poses a real theological problem for us, a serious contradiction. How can God impose on a leader the importance of relying on Him by faith (rather than the human pride of self-reliance in numbering the subjects under your rule), then "move" David to sin by inciting him to number the people? This would violate all other written scripture about God's nature! Also, when we research the same account of David taking the census as written in **1 Chronicles 21:1**, we find it was "Satan" who moved David to number Israel. In addition, James 1:13 confirms that God cannot sin, nor tempt anyone to sin. This was the first time in scripture that the formal name of "Satan" is introduced. Therefore, the "Anger of the Lord" and "Satan" then, are often interchangeable in scripture. And the Lord does not tempt us to sin. This concept is necessary in study of this chapter and more will be said about this particular finding later.

As I read about the character of Moses, it became apparent to me that he may have suffered from much the same demise as some of the jail inmates I mentioned earlier. If you evaluate his life, even with his intimate experience with the shekinah[1] glory of God, he still had a problem with anger. The scripture tells us that about the age of 40, he killed an Egyptian, whom he saw mistreating one of his fellow Hebrew. Upon his descent from the holy mountain, finding the Israelites engaged in immoral revelry and worshiping the golden calf, he again responded with uncontrolled anger by breaking the Ten Commandments written with the "finger of God." While the Israelites were wondering in the wilderness, and were again without water, he disobeyed God's commandment by striking the rock

---
[1]

rather than speaking to it to bring forth water. This act of uncontrolled anger cost him the opportunity to enter the "promised land." I believe there are many other areas of scripture that reveal this deep seeded anger that Moses had as a result of the corrupt father/child relationship.

So, to begin this examination of Moses' life as it related to God as a "Father," we start by comparing some events written by Moses' own hand with other scripture. In Acts 7:18–20 it mentions that he was "nurtured 3 months in his father's home." Contrast this with account in **Exodus 2:2** that "she hid him 3 months." Personally, I don't believe it was purely a coincidence that the book of Acts focused on the fact he was "nurtured" and "in his father's home," while Moses' account in Exodus only mentioned that his mother "hid" him when commenting on his first 3 months. Why did Moses not use either the word "nurtured," or speak of the "father," rather only the mother? Or the flip side, why did the "God inspired" writer of Acts (possibly Luke, a doctor) identify "nurtured" and "father's home, in contrast to the Torah, written by Moses?"

In light of this speculation, in examining a flood of other scriptures, know that Moses, who wrote these first 5 books of the Bible, also provided additional insight. For Moses to not mention his father's reference except in only two verses, would not be insignificant. Throughout the Torah he clearly chose not to write about or mention his father's name! This is interesting, because Moses' own writings were very careful to write the lineage of all 12 tribes from Adam to the time of the writings. He did write of his father's lineage in **Exodus 6:20** and in **Numbers 3:19** as being Amram, but to my knowledge, it's not mentioned again. It's unclear of whether he knew of his father before the exodus, or learned of him during the 40 plus years of wondering through the wilderness. Not to mention him again is odd, especially since Amram lived 137 years, and at least 40 of those years were with Moses in the wilderness. As well as another 40 years while the Israelites were in captivity in Egypt under Pharaoh. So, a total of 80 years of community proximity. His brother and sister (Aaron and Miriam) both were mentioned often and were also very involved in the events with Moses during the exodus period.

Hebrew culture has always considered it very important to maintain the father connection when identifying lineage. Therefore, as many people had the same name, but no last name as in today's culture, when identifying one person from another, one would say "David the son of Jesse." In addition, it should be mentioned that when Moses outlined the lineage of the 12 tribes of Israel, during the first 5 chapters of Leviticus alone, the term "by" or "according" "to his father's household" was mentioned 34 times! This could be a cultural reference, because cultural traditions in that time period, placed more value on the male than the female. Not because it was ordained by God, but because the family's existence was dependent on ability of the male to provide protection, sustenance to survive and prosper. One of many cultural reasons of that period.

Think about it, 34 times the term "by" or "according" "to his father's household" was mentioned! As this is from God's word and Moses was operating and writing "as the LORD commanded," I believe God was communicating something more. The Father's influence on the next generation's life was of extreme and lasting significance! Especially in relation to an identity. I am by no means an expert in the field of human development, and it's not popular in today's culture, but there are many studies that indicate the child gets most of their identity from the father role model.[2]

The second thing to consider, is that in the human race there seems to be an insatiable drive for a person to want to know from whom their identity came, especially from the father. Hollywood exposes this as well. In Star Wars movie series, Luke was in endless search of his father. In the "Pretender," Jarrod wondered from place to place playing different occupational characters, always in search of his father. Superman was in a quest for his father. In "Supernatural," the brothers estranged from their father are in search for him in every episode. "Joe Dirt" was in search of his parents. These are just a few of many examples. It's also very interesting a pattern that "Hollywood" has pursued over the last 10-20 years (after 2001 or so), in elevating the woman to be the hero of the movie or sitcom, and the male "father" role has been reduced to a weak bumbling idiot, or sinister in nature. Why the effort to eliminate or reduce the role of the "father?"

Moses, grew up in the very community where his father lived and was nurtured for the first three months by his own mother at home, in addition possibly up to a year while breast feeding in the Pharaoh daughter's custody. A total of 80 years in the same community (40 years in Egypt and 40 years in the wilderness), the connections would have been present to know who his father was. What mother would not at some point, as Moses grew older, take opportunity to tell her son who she was? Would Moses simply not care who his father might have been? What if he discovered that his father was one of those who, due to the abusive treatment of the Egyptians, exposed his son to perish to save his own life as described in **Acts 7:19**? How would Moses feel if he discovered this about his father? Would he feel loved and accepted or despised and rejected? Is it possible that since Moses wrote this book he chose to deliberately not mention his father's name? We cannot know for sure, but in light of other known facts, this may be a strong possibility.

There are some passages that provide us significant insight about Moses' childhood and how his environment and education affected his character. Beginning in **Acts 7:20–25**, verse 20 tells us he was "nurtured 3 months in his father's house." This indicates to us he really had no father other than this brief period. In verse 21, "Pharaoh's daughter nurtured him as her own," again reinforcing the point that there was no father. This point is again addressed in **Hebrews 11:24,** and also in **Exodus 2:9&10.**

**Hebrews 11:24**
**24 By faith Moses, when he had grown up, refused to be called the son of Pharaoh's daughter." (NASB)**

It's apparent here that Moses made a conscious choice to reject Pharaoh's daughter as his mother here. We can only speculate about the real reason, but I think it would be safe to assume that either there had to be an absence of the normal bonding that takes place between mother and child during those childhood years, or possibly, there was physical, mental, or emotional abuse. Looking at **Exodus 2:9–10** provides additional insight on this subject.

**Exodus 2:9–10**
**9 Then Pharaoh's daughter said to her, "Take this child away and nurse him for me and I will give you your wages." So the woman took the child and nursed him.**
**10 The child grew, and she brought him to Pharaoh's daughter and he became her son. And she named him Moses, and said, "Because I drew him out of the water." (NASB)**

It appears at the reading of this passage that Pharaoh's daughter not only couldn't nurse the child herself (at least from the breast), but didn't want to. Notice the way it's worded, "Take this child away," instead of, "come to us and nurse this child." The word for "took" in verse 9 where it says," and the woman **took** the child, and nursed it," actually means to take away; carry away. In other words, Pharaoh's daughter didn't want to be bothered with the unpleasant task of sacrificing sleep, time, and other self-centered desires to take care of this infant. "I'll pay someone else to do the undesirable stuff." The appearance is that Moses was viewed by the Pharaoh's daughter as more of a toy than a son.

**After** the child grew, the mother brought him to Pharaoh's daughter, and he became her son. The indication in the reference "after" was that the child stayed in the care of the natural mother for probably at least a year. I love my children and grandchildren dearly, but I noticed some personal preferences as they grew in relation to time I desired to spend with them. Not that "all men are alike," or even more frightening…that they are like me personally, I noticed I didn't have a great deal of interest in spending a lot of time with them until they got past the first year or so, for obvious reasons (sleep, eat, poop, repeat). However, once the child became more alive in the expression of their personality and communication efforts, I couldn't get enough of them. They were more fun! In spite of the inadequacies of Pharaoh's daughter and the difficult pain the real mother and father felt from losing their son, Moses' real mother got the joy of bonding with her son and even got paid for it! Isn't God a merciful and good God, with a sense of humor? Again, "After the child grew" indicates potentially a number of years in time frame.

**Acts 7:22**
**22 "And Moses was educated in all the learning of the Egyptians, and he was a man of power in words and deeds"** (NASB)

In comparing the verses in **Acts 7:22** and **Exodus 4:10** they indicate he was not only well educated with the best wisdom the Egyptian culture of that day had to offer, but that he was also very gifted by God in having powerful character traits. Now notice what Moses said about himself on this same subject in **Exodus 4:10**.

**Exodus 4:10**
**10 "And Moses said unto Jehovah, "Oh, Lord, I am not eloquent, neither recently nor in time past, nor since thou hast spoken to thy servant; for I am slow of speech, and of a slow tongue."** (NASB)

This verse in Exodus 4 at first glance seems to be contradictory to the character that is painted for us in **Acts 7:22**. Moses wrote this description of himself, which tells us something about how he viewed himself. However, deeper examination of the word meanings in the original language these passages were written in **Exodus 4:10** and **Acts 7:22** give us more a complete understanding, and resolves this apparent contradiction.

The word for **speech** is "peh" which means—the mouth as the means of blowing; speech, command, mind, mouth, part, portion, sentence, sound, two-edged, spoken, talk.

Moses was **"slow of speech."** This word appears to indicate that Moses had difficulty "blowing sounds, sentences, using his mouth, connecting thoughts to sentences, words, etc." In other words, he stuttered!

The word for tongue is "ishonah" which means "a fork of flame, evil speaker, language, talker; from the root word meaning to culminate, accuse, slander."

Moses was **"slow of tongue."** He was not quick to slander, speak evil of or accuse someone else. This word may also indicate that he was not very witty, or quick to return fire when in a debate, in other words he spoke rather slowly. This could also refer to an inability to confront with authority, accuse or speak harshly to, reprimand or rebuke.

But didn't **Acts 7:22** just indicate that he was powerful in word and deed? Yes it did, but in looking at the meaning of those Greek words used, we get a better understanding of this apparent contradiction. And this also gives us great insight to Moses' character and God's plan to shape him for the task of being God's chosen instrument to redeem the Israelites from captivity.

The Greek for **"word"** is "logos" which refers more to the reasoning or mental faculty; also motive, divine expression, doctrine, topic.

He was **"powerful in word and deed."** He was **powerful**, or at least capable, exceptional in his reasoning ability. He was given divine understanding, and had exceptional discerning abilities. He was capable of learning sound doctrine, and theology. The word for **deeds** simply means "action or labor." He was a capable hard worker. He strived to complete a task. He likely worked hard to gain approval. So in overview of his character he was gifted in divine understanding, had exceptional reasoning and discerning abilities, was able to be taught sound doctrine, was a hard worker, maybe even a perfectionist.

But he also stuttered, was slow to speak, had difficulty being authoritative in his speech, and was reluctant to command, reprimand, rebuke, or accuse someone. Especially to an authority figure such as Pharaoh! **Exodus 4:10** also tells us he was never "eloquent" in speech. The Hebrew here is actually two words that we translate in English as eloquent. The first word pertains to speech, the second pertains to an average person, nothing special, plain. Moses didn't think very highly of himself (which we will talk more of later), but remember that Moses wrote this book. In any case, he made judgement about his own character in this way.

If he was trained in "**all** the learning of the Egyptians" culture, why could he not speak well? He was instructed in the royal house by the best royal teachers of the kingdom. Why did he stutter? As I prayed, studied scripture and researched information about the subject of speech impediments, and stuttering, I am led to believe that all the previous perceptions of Moses as a son who was in line to be an Egyptian leader or even a respected royal family member is totally false. This view has been taught and we have seen it in such movies as "The Ten Commandments" and "The Prince of Egypt." Since I'm sure this is as new to you as it was to me, in view of the overwhelming consensus of people, even religious leaders, who believe this to be the case, please allow me to outline why I suspect differently.

As I researched the subject of speech impediments and more specifically "stuttering," I found that there were several causes, but there were usually two main causes. They could have been born with a physical defect, such as a lisp, cleft palate, or something similar. This is one cause. The other, especially more in the case of stuttering, could be the result of inadequate training in the language or a result of physical, mental and/or emotional abuse. The latter was by far the more frequent cause. Could Moses have been physically, emotionally and mentally abused? I believe there is scriptural evidence to support this possibility. It is slight, and I am being speculative, but it makes perfect sense when we look at scripture as a whole and apply this assumption to Moses' character throughout all that's written about him, and his reaction to different situations as a leader of the Israelite people. Looking again at the passage in **Acts 7:18–19** we notice additional evidentiary support.

> **Acts 7:18–19**
> **18 "Until there arose another king over Egypt who knew nothing about Joseph.**
> **19 It was he who took shrewd advantage of our race, and <u>mistreated</u> our fathers, so that they would expose their infants and they would not survive." (NASB)**

This word for **"mistreated"** is the Greek word "kakoo," which means "to injure, entreat evil, harm, exasperate. Exasperate means to enrage, irritate, to make worse, provoke." This verse informs us that this new Egyptian ruler would be of a new line of Pharaoh's that treated the Israelites with great harm and evil. This treatment was designed to provoke them ("the fathers") to enrage with anger. This treatment was so intense that the fathers became willing to expose their own children to death to avoid greater Egyptian oppression, thus resulting in controlling the increase in the Hebrew male population. This is to prevent a militant uprising against the Egyptian ruling class. **The fathers were in fact desensitized from the natural** tendency to love and protect their own children, but instead, conditioned toward a willingness to expose their own child to death. Moses was born during this period, and his father was under these influential pressures! Moses very likely witnessed a great deal of physical abuse during his youth. We already knew from scripture they beat the foremen over the Hebrew slaves. We'll look more on this in the following chapters.

Not to incite controversy or to pass judgement, but it is a fact of historical accuracy that in times past, human oppression very similar to this has occurred multiple times for many different reasons. The treatment of Israelite boys born (or more accurately, killed) during Herod's reign at the time of Jesus' birth, and more recently WWII/Hitler era in the holocaust treatment of the Jewish people. An estimated 6 million were massacred in gas furnaces and many other horrible methods of torture and death. In our own culture today, in order to satisfy an addiction to pursue selfish pleasure and prosperity, abortion or neglect of the parent/child relationship and responsibility is rampant. This is being mentioned only to set the stage to better understand how these conditions might have affected Moses' emotional state during these impressionable years of his youth.

This personal conclusion is speculative, but I believe scripture does give us confirmation about a more likely relationship between Moses and one of the more influential father figures he may have had. Parents of blended families have also realized, it is very difficult to love a stepchild as your very own, even when there is a great desire to do so. When couples re-marry into a new family relationship, often they begin with hopes of pleasing the new spouse by being a great step-parent for their child. As difficulties arise (rejection, sibling rivalry, disrespect, etc...), the wish and expectation to make the effort to love and bless another person's child can (and often does) become diminished. In addition, If both natural-born and step children are both involved, even though there is initially a strong desire to build a relationship with the new step-child, we often find ourselves giving preferential treatment to our own child over the step-child. This can be overcome, but it is difficult and I believe it requires Christ's Spirit to empower us and teach us. **If it is very difficult for those of us who desire to love a stepchild as our own, how much more difficult would it be for a person like Pharaoh, who didn't even seek the relationship?**

Now comes the cataclysmic event that begins to unravel Moses' status quo and sets in motion the preparation to deliver the Israelites from bondage of the Egyptians. The verbal exchange between God and Moses, and Moses' response provide a great deal of information when viewed in context with his character traits and environmental information we just examined. This passage is full of what I believe to be overwhelming evidence that begins to support this theory. Stay tuned, this will get a bit technical because the evidence presented just in this chapter alone is not enough to draw a firm conclusion. But rather the examination of the entire culmination of evidence over the course of this entire book. So, here we go…

**Exodus 2:11–14.**
**11 Now it came about in those days, when Moses had grown up, that he went out to his brethren and looked on their hard labors; and saw an Egyptian beating a Hebrew, one of his brethren.**
**12 So he looked this way and that, and when he saw that there was no one around, he struck down the Egyptian and hid him in the sand.**
**13 And he went out the second day, and, behold, two men of the Hebrews were fighting with each other: and he said to the offender, "Why are you striking your companion?"**
**14 And he said, "Who made you a prince and a judge over us? Are you intending to kill**

**me, as you killed the Egyptian?" And Moses
feared, and said, "Surely the matter has become
known."**

**15 When Pharaoh heard of this matter,
he tried to kill Moses. But Moses fled from the
presence of Pharaoh, and settled in the land
of Midian: and he sat down by a well.** (NASB)

After Moses thought he had successfully defended his fellow
Hebrew from oppression without being seen by an Egyptian, he
probably felt that his own people would have accepted him as one
of their own. More than likely, the Hebrew slave that was saved by
Moses spread the word of what had happened, and it immediately
spread like wildfire. This would only make sense as Moses, a Semitic
Jew, was being raised in a royal Egyptian (dark, olive-skinned) household, and all who saw him would know that this was a slave boy
being raised in a pampered royal home. He was likely the talk of the
territory, by both the Hebrew slave community and the Egyptian
community.

The Hebrews would have most likely despised one of their own
being spared the cruel treatment that they themselves endured and
watched of their own sons and family members, while in contrast, he
would eat the royal food and have no slave work. My belief is that
Moses, in light of human nature, wasn't very well received by his own
people. In **Acts 7:35**, in Stephen's defense speech, Stephen, <u>full of the
Holy Spirit</u>, said that the Hebrews "disowned" him.

Look at what his own Hebrew fellow man said to him in **Exodus
2:14**. If I may paraphrase, I believe he said something like this: "Oh,
yeah, right, like you're a prince (a son of the ruling class king), or a
judge (one granted authority to rule by the ruling king) over us?" I
believe this was intended as a sarcastic joke. Anyone who valued his
own life, would not dare speak to a royal prince with power in this
way, for fear of being executed for mere disrespect! It is apparent that
all the other Hebrews obviously viewed Moses as not being consid-

ered as a real son of Pharaoh, or part of the ruling political hierarchy, much less a prince. Thus, this Hebrew who was being confronted with his own guilt, tried to attack his accuser, maybe as we would be tempted to do as well, by saying the most hurtful thing you can think of. In this case, the words were to remind Moses that he was really "a nobody" in royal clothes as everyone else already knew.

The Egyptians also probably talked about him in their private circles. I doubt that Pharaoh really considered him part of the royal family in light of verse 15. If Moses really felt a part of the family as a son, he wouldn't have feared retribution from Pharaoh after killing an Egyptian commoner, at least not enough to fear for his life. Remember, in that day, the royal class rulers were considered not just rulers, but gods with supernatural gifts and powers. They were thought of as being deity, above the law.

What about the relationship between Moses and Pharaoh? It is apparent from **Exodus 2:14–15** that there was no lost love between them. Pharaoh sought to kill him, not question him to see if what he had heard was true, or discipline him as a father would a son. The relational rift between the Pharaoh and Moses was a lot greater than the spoken history generationally passed down would suggest. In verse 14 after this comment by the fellow Hebrew, Moses was overcome by fear! He immediately evaluated what the fellow Hebrew had said, thought back on his relationship to the Pharaoh and royal family. He knew immediately that the Hebrew slave was right and fled the country for fear of having provided Pharaoh a reason to end his life! He didn't just flee to the next town, but fled the entire region under Pharaoh's control. As such, Pharaoh pursued Moses in effort to kill him. This raising of a Hebrew slave as a family member could be construed as tarnishing his legacy and image of superiority among the other line of Egyptian Rulers as recorded by history, which was a really big deal among this culture. Not to mention the possible loss of respect among the people of the land.

Additional emphasis on this subject is necessary here. On a trip to Egypt recently, more specifically, Karnak, as we toured the burial chambers of the kings and listened to the guide explain what archeologists were discovering, it became apparent that most all of the Pharaoh's of that time period were always focused on their eternal legacy. Construction on their tomb or glorified burial memorial began up to 25-30 years in advance of their actual death in many cases. History of actual events were sometimes altered, eliminated, or expounded to make the Pharaoh appear more grandiose than the reality. We already know that the historic Israelite exodus was omitted from this Pharaoh's historic record, but later found as a small mention in other record.

In light of this tendency, to have a Hebrew in the royal household slay another Egyptian and the Pharaoh do little or nothing about it would place a severe threat to his eternal legacy. Should this information spread throughout the kingdom, his reputation as an all-powerful leader over the Egyptian kingdom would be in serious trouble. He could become a target of assassination or a coup. In addition, his legacy could be tainted as being weak.

Moses "when he had grown up" refused to be called the son of Pharaoh's daughter (**Hebrews 11:24**). Was this because he disliked the Pharaoh's daughter or was he rejecting the entire Egyptian race? He stuttered. One of the causes for stuttering is often physical and / or emotional abuse. This could be especially true here in light of the fact that scripture already tells us that Moses was gifted intellectually (**Acts 7:22**). Stuttering then, was most likely not a result of being slow minded.

Could Pharaoh have been abusive to Moses as a child? The Hebrews joked about him being a prince. Could they have witnessed this abuse? Remember Moses' low self-esteem as revealed in **Exodus 4:10**. This is again reinforced in other passages. In **Exodus 3:11** when God told him that he was chosen to lead the people out of Egypt he replied, "**Who am I that I should go to Pharaoh**," even though God had told him that God Himself would rescue His people and would fight the battles. Again, in **Numbers 12:3,** it tells us that "**Moses was more humble than anyone else on the face of the earth**." If a person were abused by their own family (the household of Pharaoh) and rejected by their own nationality (the Hebrews), wouldn't this person, then, begin to feel they were of no value to anyone? Wouldn't they be more humble than any man on the face of the earth? I believe this is the **real** Moses.

If a person doesn't have a father, they usually develop that role model from the next closest thing to a father. A coach, an uncle, stepfather, grandfather, media movies, television, etc... They take on father role models' character themselves. **In this book, the most important point is that we will view the character of "God the Father" in the same way we view the character and nature of our earthly role model for a father!**

Another important application was best said by Jim Craddock, founder of Scope Ministries International, a counselor who wrote and ministered exhaustively on this subject, wrote "You will view yourself and treat others in the same way that you believe God the Father views and treats you!"[3] This statement profoundly affected my life! Even more so as life's circumstances and experiences matured my understanding of its depth.

One other interesting point I want to add here. This book has been a work in progress over the last 25 years in my life. On it's final edit, the first page of this chapter was added to create a reader's interest, as the original manuscript was a bit clinical. I was moved to write about personal memories that drew the reader into the subject matter of the book. The opening paragraph talked about a church that was often in the media limelight for harsh incendiary slogans regarding homosexual issues facing our culture. After writing this paragraph, I decided to research the church organization. I discov-

---

3

ered that it's founder who said, "it was his sacred duty to warn others of God's anger," had 13 children that made up a large segment of the members. His own son gave accounts that revealed that their father ABUSED HIS CHILDREN AND HIS WIFE to maintain his authority.

While this chapter focused on the character of Moses, this book is about the character of "God the Father!" In keeping with this pursuit, as we proceed through the events of Moses' life, we should be keeping our focus on how God interacted with Moses in these events to glean from them what God the Father's character is really like, and how He relates to us! There are a few important applications this chapter reveals about God the Father's character. During the course of this chapter we noticed that when speaking to Moses, God referred to Himself 4 times as "the God of your Fathers." There are at least two main points we can draw from this.

The first is to understand that God was expressing His character as that of being a timeless eternal God. "The God of your fathers" referred to fathers of several generations (no beginning ... and no end)! He is the same God that has been intimately interacting with all of humanity from the beginning, especially of the culture of Moses' period and all of the founding forefathers who wrote "inspired" word of God.

The second point is based on the assumption that the evidence used to support Moses' character as outlined in chapter 1 is correct. He was deeply wounded by the rejection of both the Hebrews and the Egyptians. The pain caused by the discovery of Moses' natural father possibly leaving him to die, coupled with the extreme corruption of other earthly male/father figure role models he may have been exposed could have left him with an extremely low self-esteem, so much it affected his ability to speak (stuttering), and feeling unacceptable by everyone, even his own race.

With this in mind, the term God used repeatedly when speaking to Moses about Himself being THE GOD who is also a Father, could have drawn Moses into a desire to experience the most important relationship he had been longing for. A Father /Son relationship. Is essence, to use Moses' greatest longing in order enable Moses to discover an identity, and an acceptance by a father. His father.

God used the tragedy of Moses' life to shape a character of humility, which was necessary before God could use Moses to set His people free and be the instrument of mighty miracles. The man who God chose was a murderer, had a deep seeded problem with anger, possessed **a very** poor self-esteem, felt rejected by his people, stuttered; and was afraid to confront and/or engage in the rebuke of an authority figure, especially a king/god of a Kingdom!

For God to use a man of mighty character strength, and political power, would have diverted attention away from God and toward a mere man. This was contrary to what God is trying to show the world. That He is, in fact, "The Almighty God!" Able to take the weakest and most unlikely person and bring about a miraculous event. This is more consistent with the way God has historically interacted with humanity throughout all of scripture, as well. Using the weakest to carry out the greatest acts (the disciples, King David, Rahab, the harlot, the 12 disciples, etc…) To free the Israelites, when they were least able to free themselves, even with an uprising. They were beat down and disillusioned. They had given up on life and their own strength, thus they were crying out to God to save them. We too, usually don't cry out to God to save us until we have utterly exhausted all of our own hopes and strengths. Can God use tragedies in your life to accomplish His will for your life as well? He can!

In the next few chapters we will see, I believe, what kind of earthly role model Moses had as a father by the way Moses responded to the Israelites. God pursued Moses to teach him who "God the Father" really is through this process of leading the people to freedom. As we look together at this, pray that God will reveal to you areas of your own life in which you have a corrupted view of God the Father's character. Understanding our own view of God and how it was shaped by our earthly father relationship, the media, and other male role models that influenced us. Allow Christ to reveal to us the true character of "God the Father" as He truly is.

Here are other Related Scriptures to explore.
**Proverbs 22:4, 29:23 Isaiah 57:15 James 4:10 1 Peter 5:5**

1 "Shekinah"—(In Jewish and Christian theology)
the glory of the divine presence, conventionally
represented as light or interpreted symbolically.
Oxford Dictionaries
2 The Effects of Father Involvement: An Updated Research
Summary of the Evidence Sarah Allen, PhD and Kerry Daly, PhD
University of Guelph May 2000
3 Jim Craddock, Scope Ministries International Inc
"Pneumanetics" "Be Transformed" "FatherCare"

# TRAIL OF TEARS

WHEN I READ ABOUT THE patriarchs of the Bible, I had the assumption they must have known "God" from birth. For God to use them to make such a permanent mark on humanity for all time, surely, they had to be some special kind of "holy" person. In Europe, there's a magnificent cathedral for every major apostle. Even Stephen had one in Vienna. It was memorable because there was hundreds of these rocks hanging from this beautifully ornate cathedral ceiling. Moses is carved on the Library of Congress in Washington DC, and his portrait is inscribed on the US Chamber of the House of Representatives. To consider the possibility Moses didn't even know or worship the God of the Hebrews when he encountered the Almighty God in the burning bush was unthinkable. Is this possible? Would God consider asking someone who never even knew or worshipped Him to deliver His people from Egypt? As strange as this seems, I believe it's a very strong possibility.

I know the first chapters had to rely on a fair amount of speculation about Moses's character. This chapter will take some speculative liberty as well. However, as you piece all the speculations together with the mounting scriptural evidentiary support being compounded, it becomes a lot less speculative. If these assumptions in the previous chapters are accurate, then imagine for a moment how Moses may have felt after those highly emotional events took place.

He had just experienced forty years of physical and/or emotional abuse from the Pharaoh and felt the intense pain of rejection from his own people, the Israelites. I'm sure, as he was walking, perhaps running, through the desert in fear of the Pharaoh's pursuit, reflecting on his pain and loneliness. He would have felt unloved and unacceptable to everyone. Satan, referred to by the Scripture as the

"the accuser" (**Revelation 12:10; Zachariah 3:1–2**), may have been interjecting thoughts upon Moses accusing him of being a murderer and causing him to feel he was unacceptable, even to God. I believe it's very possible at this point of Moses's life that he may not have even worshipped the God of the Israelites. Putting distance between himself and the ones from Egypt who were in pursuit to kill him and establishing a peaceful family life in the land of Midian likely would've brought relief and even a joy of life to his soul.

**Exodus 2:15–25** describes for us the immediate events that followed his departure from Egypt. He wandered to the land of Midian and sat down by a well. Trying not to read too much into this biblical account, I can't help but imagine that he is exhausted physically, mentally, and emotionally. He finds this well in the desert and just collapses to gather his thoughts and rest. There he meets the seven daughters of a man named Reuel, who is the priest of Midian. Moses helps and protects these daughters from other shepherds in the territory. Upon hearing of this, Reuel sends for Moses and offers his daughter Zipporah as his wife. Moses marries and has two children. For the next forty years through his family in Midian, Moses may have found more love and acceptance than he had ever previously experienced. This period of his life provided relief and healing to some degree from the tragedy of Egypt.

Moses is now about eighty years old (**Acts 7:23, 30**), and the Pharaoh who was seeking to kill Moses has died. Moses encounters the strangest sight when the "angel of the Lord" appeared in the burning bush on Mount Sinai. In light of my speculation of his experience with his own Hebrew people, and treatment from the Egyptians, he was probably not all that excited about hearing from the LORD that he was chosen to go back to Egypt to be the deliverer of the Hebrews. In fact, I am sure there were many emotions that welled up at that very moment. Fear, dread, and anger were probably the major ones.

Moses who was "slow of speech" and "slow of tongue" (*slow to accuse, rebuke, slander*) didn't have the characteristics necessary to be an attorney or debater. He has suddenly found himself in the debate of his life. This debate was with none other than the "Almighty God"!

He began presenting his case with all the reasons he shouldn't be the one chosen to lead the Israelites from captivity in Egypt.

> The LORD said, "I have surely seen the affliction of My people who are in Egypt, and have given heed to their cry because of their taskmasters, for I am aware of their sufferings.
> So I have come down to deliver them from the power of the Egyptians, and to bring them up from that land to a good and spacious land, to a land flowing with milk and honey, to the place of the Canaanite and the Hittite and the Amorite and the Perizzite and the Hivite and the Jebusite.
> Now, behold, the cry of the sons of Israel has come to Me; furthermore, I have seen the oppression with which the Egyptians are oppressing them.
> Therefore, come now, and I will send you to Pharaoh, so that you may bring My people, the sons of Israel, out of Egypt." (Exodus 3:7–10 NASB)

The Lord expressed twice to Moses (verses 7 and 9) His character of love and compassion toward the Israelites, informing Moses that He had heard their cries and had seen their harsh oppression and sufferings. Why twice? Could God be placing an emphasis on this aspect of His character for a designed purpose in speaking with Moses? Why did Moses kill the Egyptian in defending his fellow Hebrew? Moses was a witness to the oppression and suffering. Moses also had a heart of compassion for his own people. Remember how he protected the seven daughters of Midian from the shepherds. I believe God was appealing to Moses's heart of compassion that was already present in his character. I believe God was gently reasoning with Moses, being understanding of his deep fear and hurt. Then comes Moses's first line of argument.

> **But Moses said to God, "Who am I, that I should go to Pharaoh, and that I should bring the sons of Israel out of Egypt?"** (Exodus 3:11 NASB)

Moses was sure that God was unaware how inadequate he was for the job, considering all the others God could have chosen. Surely, God had missed seeing the way he and the Pharaoh had related to each other. Remember two of the things we discovered about Moses's character: he was "slow of speech" (he stuttered) and was "slow of tongue" (he had difficulty confronting authority, or being able to accuse, slander, rebuke, debate—"fork of flame"). To Moses, it was obvious that God had overlooked these flaws in choosing him for the task. Moses also had low self-esteem. He believed he was a "nobody." At this point in his life, he didn't believe in God or himself!

> **And He said, "Certainly I will be with you, and this shall be the sign to you that it is I who have sent you: when you have brought the people out of Egypt, you shall worship God at this mountain."** (Exodus 3:12 NASB)

God's reply was to reassure Moses that He would go with him and be the source of power that delivers the people from the Pharaoh's bondage. God was not relying on Moses's own ability. Moses responds.

> **Then Moses said to God, "Behold, I am going to the sons of Israel, and I will say to them, 'The God of your fathers has sent me to you.' Now they may say to me, 'What is His name?' What shall I say to them?"** (Exodus 3:13 NASB)

This may seem like a silly question when Moses, playing the devil's advocate, says, "When they ask me, 'What is his name?' what shall I say?" Here, it may be helpful to understand the Egyptian culture in a bit more detail. They worshipped many different gods, depending upon what they were needing at the time. They had a god of war, a god of fertility, a god of love, sun, moon, stars, etc. The fact that He had to ask, "What is his name?" is probably an indication that Moses didn't really know the God of Israel personally at this time, at least not intimately. There was no mention in the Scripture of any interaction between God and Moses prior to this time. Moses, being "educated in all the learning of the Egyptians" (**Acts 7:22**), would have naturally responded, if I may paraphrase, "Which god is sending me?" As a side note, this was the reason the fire burned without consuming the bush. No other "god" of Egypt could accomplish this feat.

> **God said to Moses, "I AM WHO I AM"; and He said, "Thus you shall say to the sons of Israel, 'I AM has sent me to you.'"**
> **God, furthermore, said to Moses, "Thus you shall say to the sons of Israel, 'The LORD, the God of your fathers, the God of Abraham, the God of Isaac, and the God of Jacob, has sent me to you.' This is My name forever, and this is My memorial-name to all generations.**
> (Exodus 3:14–15 NASB)

Here, God makes sure that Moses knows who He is. The **"I AM."** The only God, Creator God of all that exists, the Eternal God of all gods, the God of all generations (Abraham, Isaac, Jacob). The God of the people you desired to be accepted by, the God of your fathers. My name is **"JEHOVAH."** The God of the Hebrews. In a sense, I believe God was gently teaching Moses who He is. I believe the statement "God of your fathers" is further evidence that Moses didn't already have an intimate relationship with God. Even what he had been taught about the Hebrew God may have been limited. Moses's education was of the Egyptians, not Hebrew culture. So a proper introduction and teaching may have been necessary here.

Another interesting note to mention is that God tells Moses to inform the Israelites that God is sending him to them (not to the Pharaoh). I originally thought God would be concerned with addressing the one who controlled the power to hold the people in captivity or set them free. Once God declares something, it will happen! Man's physical and mental limitations do not matter. God also tends to send word to His chosen ahead of what He's about to do before He does it! He's always trying to build our faith in Him. God is preparing Moses to lead the people and condition the people to follow Moses as the face of God's chosen deliverer.

During my childhood years, I believed Moses already knew God and was just being argumentative here. I most likely thought this way because my father was a pastor. Fortunately, I always knew about the LORD and assumed everyone else did too. Moses may very well have known <u>of</u> God, but it appears he may not have known God intimately. The psalmist spoke about this very thing in **Psalm 103:7** in which he differentiated between knowing God intimately (His ways) as Moses learned later and just knowing "of" Him (His acts) as the sons of Israel did. Chronologically, Moses had not yet experienced the miracles of God, outside the burning bush.

I also used to believe that God was yelling at Moses when He said, **"I AM WHO I AM. Tell them I AM has sent me to you."** As I wondered about why I thought this way about God, I immediately thought about the scene in the Charlton Heston movie *The Ten Commandments*. As I remember it, when God spoke those words in the movie, His voice boomed, as if He was yelling at Moses. That scene, corrupted by man's interpretation, shaped the way I viewed God throughout life. The media has incredible power like that. To understand God's character as He really is requires us to know His word on these subjects and make a choice to believe God's word instead of what past influences have done to shape our view of Him.

**Isaiah 42:2** tells us when speaking about Christ that **"He will not cry out or raise his voice, nor make his voice heard in the street."** In the next chapter, I discuss the character of Christ and that of God the Father are interchangeable (**John 5:19, 12:45, 14:7 and chapters 8, 9, 11**). God wasn't yelling at Moses but was properly introducing Himself, making sure Moses knew the difference between the Only True God and other so-called gods. Why did I believe that God was loud? Even though my father was one of the most patient men I've ever known, he sometimes yelled when he became irritated. Humans are impatient, but God is patient. We yell, thinking it makes us bigger or more powerful or we can force our point over someone else's voice. God knows who He is and doesn't need to yell. He can make His thoughts known without uttering a word.

Gently and lovingly, God builds Moses's assurance of His power and willingness to support every step in this process. The miracles done in Moses's presence (Exodus 4) would have to build his confidence. Living by faith in His Word does the same thing for us. Do you know His ways or just about His acts? It's a constant truth, because God Himself takes the responsibility to build our faith! God cannot fail! **Philippians 1:6** says, "*For I am* confident of this very thing, that He who began a good work in you will perfect it until the day of Christ Jesus" (NASB; emphasis mine).

Notice God told Moses to gather the Israelite elders together and go "ask," not go "tell," the Pharaoh to let the Israelites go. Look at how they were to speak to the Pharaoh in **Exodus 3:18: "So now, please, let us go a three days' journey…"** Why would the "Almighty God" of the universe need to ask, **"Please, let us go"**? This shows God's respect for all of humanity, created "in His image," including the Pharaoh. God already knew what the outcome was going to be, but He was **teaching** Moses a way of engaging with people (especially our enemies) in a way that he probably hadn't considered before. Remember whom he learned from—the Pharaoh, who considered himself a deity and ruled oppressively over all other people. Do you think the Pharaoh asked "please" when he wanted something? I doubt it.

There are two things God is careful to communicate to Moses in this next passage in **Exodus 3:15–16.** First, God spent time reassuring Moses that He is an eternal, living God. Twice, He mentions He is (present tense) the God of Abraham, Isaac, and Jacob. Second, He mentions He is a caring God in **verse 16.** Here, He tells Moses to gather the elders of Israel and tell them, **"I am indeed concerned about you, and what has been done to you in Egypt."** He also confirms to Moses what He is going to do for the Israelites after they leave Egypt. He had a plan to bring them into a fertile and spacious land. He also confirmed to Moses that it would be God's power that would bring it about. <u>God is indeed concerned about **us** as well!</u> He also has a long-term plan for our lives (**Jeremiah 29:11** and **33:3**).

> **So I will stretch out My hand and strike Egypt with all My miracles which I shall do in the midst of it; and after that he will let you go.** (NASB)

> **Then Moses said, "What if they will not believe me or listen to what I say? For they may say, 'The Lord has not appeared to you.'"** (Exodus 4:1 NASB)

Moses continues asking questions in **Exodus 4:1**. I've known people like that, a million questions! They just keep asking them, looking for a way to self-destruct the plan. It drives me crazy, but I digress. If you think back to the last time Moses attempted to help his people, you can easily understand why he would ask God this question: "What if they don't believe me or listen to what I say?" They rejected his help and turned against him. Moses was well aware of how the Israelites were. God responded in **Exodus 4:2–9** by revealing firsthand His power (the miracles). Seeing is believing! Moses now knows God's power is sufficient to do what He said He would do in **Exodus 3:20**. You would think after this display of power Moses would be willing to agree with God and say, "Let's go get 'em, LORD, You and me!" But this was not the case.

> **Then Moses said to the Lord, "Please, Lord, I have never been eloquent, neither recently nor in time past, nor since You have**

**spoken to Your servant; for I am slow of speech and slow of tongue."**

**The Lord said to him, "Who has made man's mouth? Or who makes *him* mute or deaf, or seeing or blind? Is it not I, the Lord?**

**Now then go, and I, even I, will be with your mouth, and teach you what you are to say."**

**But he said, "Please, Lord, now send *the message* by whomever You will."** (Exodus 4:10–13 NASB)

Even in light of the powerful miracles God just performed to reassure him, Moses was still looking at his own ability rather than God's to determine the probability of success. We can speculate on several reasons for this. It may have been out of fear. He was rejected by the Israelites once, and the pain was intense. Don't we respond in the same way? If you have been a victim of divorce, the natural tendency is to attempt to become self-sufficient and withdrawn to avoid the pain, just in case the next relationship fails. In reality though, refusing to open yourself up to your new spouse (being vulnerable) is generally a sure recipe for another failed marriage because the new spouse who is already sensitive to rejection perceives your withdrawn and untrusting actions as a rejection of them personally. If we will learn to trust God for our protection, needs, and welfare, then we can find strength to be vulnerable toward others, **even to those that we believe would be inclined to harm us!** Isn't God more powerful than they? Hasn't He made us promises? Or do you not believe Him? He's got our back!

Maybe Moses's already-low self-esteem had him trapped or deceived him into believing even God couldn't or wouldn't help him. It's often easy to believe God can or desires to help or change others, but we often feel He won't help or change us. Do you think Moses's relationship with the Pharaoh (his role model for a father) left him without the confidence to trust that God would do what He said He would do? Or even that God had Moses's best interest at heart? Moses feared! He felt he was in a no-win situation. God (like the Pharaoh) was more powerful than Moses. Therefore, if he obeyed God and failed, what would happen? Would God be angry with Moses like the Pharaoh was angry with him? If he disobeyed God, would this powerful God seek to kill him?

I believe Moses wished God would just leave him alone to enjoy the life he had found for himself and just not take the risk. How many of us have decided to do the same with our own life? God had a better plan. Again (in **verse 11**), God patiently reasoned with Moses, assuring him that He is the Creator and upholds all existence with His right hand. God is still trying to teach Moses what kind of God and Father He is. He desires to teach us His character as well.

Have you experienced God's power in ways that have reassured you of who He really is? If not, then you too may not really know God intimately. God desires us to know Him intimately just as Moses, other Bible characters, and believers have before you. He is waiting patiently for you to trust Him by faith so that we may provide Him a stage to show Himself faithful, powerful, and loving toward you. God is not a respecter of persons but is equal and loving toward all who will seek Him. If you truly know Him intimately (His ways), then you have seen His miraculous works already. If you just know of Him (His acts), then you have only heard of His miraculous works but not really experienced them in your own life.

Moses was still not able to trust God fully as indicated in **verse 13**. If I may paraphrase, "Please, Lord, send the message by anyone you choose, just not me." God again responded.

> **Then the anger of the Lord burned against Moses, and He said, "Is there not your brother Aaron the Levite? I know that he speaks fluently. And moreover, behold, he is coming out to meet you; when he sees you, he will be glad in his heart.**
>
> **You are to speak to him and put the words in his mouth; and I, even I, will be with your**

**mouth and his mouth, and I will teach you
what you are to do.**

**Moreover, he shall speak for you to the
people; and he will be as a mouth for you and
you will be as God to him.**

**You shall take in your hand this staff, with
which you shall perform the signs."** (Exodus
4:14–17 NASB)

When you read these verses again very carefully and only look
at what God actually said, does it really sound like God is angry
with Moses? In verse 14, God mentions Moses's brother, Aaron. He
assured Moses that Aaron "speaks fluently" and even suggested that
Aaron would be "glad in his heart" to see him. Does this sound like
an angry God speaking to Moses in this exchange? Again, in keeping
with the understanding that God's word is the best interpreter of
itself, reading **Isaiah 54:9** provides additional clarity in the discern-
ment of scriptural events. Keep in mind, Moses wrote the first five
books of the Old Testament and would have written about God the
way he viewed or understood God during those events. We would
write about our view of events in our own life in a journal or diary
the same way. Over time and experience, as we mature, we often
understand God and the events in a much different way.

**To me this is like the days of Noah, when
I swore that the waters of Noah would never
again cover the earth. So now I have sworn
not to be angry with you, never to rebuke you
again. (Isaiah 54:9 ASV)**

This verse tells us that God has sworn not to be angry with
His people again (since the flood). The great flood occurred before
Moses's time. Think about Jesus, who is the "I Am" that was inter-
acting with Moses here. How did Jesus respond when the disciples
failed? How did he respond when Peter denied Him three times?
When He was being beaten and unjustly crucified (**Luke 23:34**)?

Was God angry here with Moses? Since He is a God who is all-know-ing, wouldn't He be aware of Moses's past experiences and how that pain may have damaged his perception and understanding of God's true character? The Scripture says that God is a compassionate God (**Deuteronomy 4:31; Lamentations 3:22; James 5:11**), a patient God (**2 Peter 3:9**), full of loving-kindness and mercy (**Psalm 86:15**). If He were angry here, wouldn't that be contradictory to all of what the Scripture tells us about God? I believe it would.

My belief is that Moses, the author of this book, <u>believed</u> God was angry with him, as he was only responding to how all other male, "father figure" role models had previously reacted toward him in similar circumstances. Therefore, he wrote about God with the perception he had of God at that time in his life.

As we will discover later in this book, Moses's view of God changed as God continued to reveal Himself to Moses through these events leading the Israelites to freedom from Egyptian bondage.

Carefully reviewing what God said in **Exodus 4:14–17**, it appears that God may have expressed something more like (again, personal paraphrasing) "Okay, Moses, I understand your hurt, fear, and reluctance; and I know why you are unable to trust me fully. So I will take you where you are and will gently and patiently rebuild you into the person I created you to be, repairing the damage done to you along the way. See, I am already sending your brother, Aaron, because I know it would be easier for you to trust him more than anyone else, to help you. However, Moses, I will speak to <u>you</u>, and <u>you</u> will pass the words on to him because <u>you are the one</u> through which I have chosen to redeem My people. Do not be afraid, I will be with you, and <u>I will do the work</u>."

This book is designed to help us gain a better understanding of the consistency of God the Father's character throughout all of Scripture and to intimately know Him as He really is toward us. Reflect on some of the thoughts you have had about God's character in these passages prior to this presentation. Begin evaluating your previous relationships, especially father role models, and be willing to meditate in prayer how those experiences might have influenced the way you have viewed God also.

I would urge you to begin memorizing those scriptures that correct the false beliefs about God the Father's character. They affect almost every area of your life, especially your desire to rely upon and trust God. <u>I would encourage you also to pray for God to change</u> specific corrupt belief patterns that you may have of God.

# THE "I AM"

I HAVE DISCOVERED OVER THE years that many people have a difficult time understanding the relationship between God the Father, Jehovah, YHWH, the angel of the LORD, Jesus Christ, and the Holy Spirit. Some believe that Jesus is God; others believe that He is God's Son, but not God. Almost all the various religions will acknowledge Jesus's life, crucifixion, and renowned human relational behavior modeled to the world. Many believe Jesus to be a great prophet, wise teacher, and moral man; attest to His miracles; etc., but nothing more. It's interesting that all the world's major religions feel compelled to account for Jesus in one way or another. J. Warner Wallace has written a very well-researched expose of the different religions and their varied beliefs about the historical Jesus.[1] The following two paragraphs are a few excerpts (paraphrased) from his work.

Both ancient and modern Jews typically accept Jesus was a rabbi and popular teacher, although they would deny He is the Messiah *(The Toledot Yeshu)*. Muslims believe Jesus was to be revered as a prophet and apostle of God. Muslims also acknowledge Jesus was a divinely wise teacher (Quran 57:27), but they deny He is God, or the Son of God (Quran 5:75; Quran 9:30). Buddhists acknowledge Jesus as a "wise teacher" (the fourteenth Dalai Lama, Tenzin Gyatso, has even recognized Jesus as a "bodhisattva"—one who dedicates his life sacrificially to the service and betterment of others), a "holy man" (the current Dalai Lama), and an "enlightened man" (fourteenth-century Zen master, Gasan Jōseki). He is not seen as divine. Judaism, Islam, Buddhists, and followers of the Baha'i faith all acknowledge Jesus's miracles.

"Hindus are willing to acknowledge Jesus as divine. However, He is not seen as "uniquely" divine. Hindus often worship many gods and goddesses and are eager to include Jesus in their list of deities. However, most Hindus don't see Jesus as the "only" way to God. Instead, some understand Jesus as the perfect example of "self-realization" (the goal of Hindu "dharma"). While some Hindus may sort of see Jesus as "a" God-man, they would also list other "God-man" examples such as Rama, Krishna, and Buddha. Jesus is simply one of many "ishtas" (forms of the divine) in the history of mankind."[2]

Even various denominations who claim adherence to the tenets of Christianity can distort Jesus's identity and authority—Jehovah's Witness, Mormon, and Christian Science, to name a few. I will address a few of these later in the chapter.

Then there are many different beliefs about the idea of the Trinity (Father, Son, and Holy Spirit). There are several reasons for this diversity. I, for one, can't think of anything in this present physical world that resembles it. There is the idea of $H_2O$ (water). It can be called steam, water, or ice as different temperatures affect it; but in the end, it's still $H_2O$. But even that doesn't properly compare to God being the Father, Son, and Spirit at the same time. He is the same yesterday, today, and forever; and different outer environments do not affect Him. Another reason is because many people lack true knowledge of what the Scriptures teach on the subject but rely instead on what they have heard from others. There is another reason that we will focus on in this chapter. In any case, what you believe about God's nature is of primary importance because it is the foundation on which your entire religious belief is based on, the nature of who God is.

I will not attempt to do a comprehensive examination of this subject in this book, because I'm not qualified to do so. However, I want to explore some of these references to God as it relates to our focus on Moses. More specifically, the "angel of the LORD" that appeared to Moses in the burning bush, and how this "angel of the LORD," Jesus Christ, and God the Father relate to one another. This is in line with continuing to discover the character of God the Father as presented to Moses.

**And the Angel of the LORD appeared to him in a blazing fire from the midst of the**

**bush; and he looked, and behold, the bush was burning with fire, yet the bush was not consumed.** (Exodus 3:2 NASB)

The word for "angel" in the term "angel of the LORD" is *ma'lak*, which has several meanings. *Strong's Concordance* translates it as "ambassador, king, angel, and messenger." It is from the root word that means "to dispatch as deputy; a messenger (specifically of God), also a prophet, priest, or teacher." The term "angel of the LORD" is used in the Scripture in many places and used in a variety of ways, sometimes referring to God; sometimes a man such as prophet, priest, or teacher; sometimes to a created angel; and even in some cases a fallen angel (demon), even as Satan. Whatever the application, understand that God uses all these to communicate and interact with mankind in this physical realm. "Who is communicating with Moses here?" This is the question we will direct the focus to.

**When the LORD saw that he turned aside to look, God called to him from the midst of the bush, and said, "Moses, Moses!" and he said, "here I am." (Exodus 3:4 NASB)**

This passage clearly states that the angel of the LORD is God Himself! Let me clarify a couple of the references given here. The first is the word "LORD." This is a sacred intimate or proper name for the Supreme God translated in English as "Jehovah." The proper Hebrew spelling is "Yahweh." However, out of fear and reverence, they removed the vowels for fear of mispronouncing His intimate name. Thus, the capital consonants remain—YHWH.

The next reference is the word for "God." This word is *Elohiym*, which is a <u>plural</u> reference to the Supreme God. The fact that it is plural is significant. In our English language, it would be correct to translate it as "Gods called to him from the midst of the bush." You might think this was a grammatical error. However, it occurs in every reference to our Holy God throughout the Scripture. Our God is then a plural God even though He says many times that He is one God (**Deuteronomy 6:4; Psalm 71:22; 2 Samuel 7:22; Isaiah 43:10; Isaiah 44:6; Mark 12:29**). He is One God with different forms, as He has revealed Himself to mankind.

> **Moreover He said, I Am the God of thy father, the God of Abraham, the God of Isaac, and the God of Jacob. And Moses hid his face; for he was afraid to look upon God.** (Exodus 3:6 KJV)

As I mentioned in the last chapter, God took great care to explain to Moses that He is an eternal God. This passage reflects the phrase He used to communicate this concept. The *God of Abraham, Isaac, Jacob* was a time reference, since all those well-known patriarchs had been dead for several hundred years. However, their legends and their history with their God had been passed down for generations. This is the same timeless God who interacted with all of them. At this point, Moses, who knew of the legends, was afraid. Who wouldn't be a little freaked out! You got this raging fire speaking to you, and the bush is not being consumed. Not a normal day, for sure.

So here, we know this "angel of the LORD" is God Himself—the Eternal Creator God, YHWH, which we translate as "Jehovah." This is the Father God that Jesus and all worshippers of ancient Israel prayed to also. This begins to unravel other difficult questions. For example, if Jesus prayed to Him, who then is Jesus? What about the scripture in **John 14:6**, in which Jesus says, **"I Am the way the truth and the life, no one comes to the Father, but through Me"**? Jesus didn't come until about one thousand five hundred years after Moses, and nearly two thousand years after Abraham. If Jesus is God, why did He pray to Himself? If Jesus isn't God, then He must be considered a liar and lunatic, for He claimed there was no other way to be saved but by Him. What about Noah, King David, the priests, prophets, and all those who lived before Christ came? Who did they swear allegiance to and worship? Before providing answers to these questions, more evidence must be outlined to fully comprehend the conclusion.

> **I have come in my Father's name, and you do not receive Me; if another comes in his own name, you will receive him.** (John 5:43 NASB; emphasis mine)

This is as compared to someone who comes to a group and introduces himself with "Hi, I'm John Smith, son of Benjamin Smith." No one will dispute or question that claim to be true. Who did Jesus claim Himself to be in **John 5:43**? Jesus was claiming He had come in God's character and authority. He was saying that He is God the Father's Son! Was He just claiming He was "a" son just like all of us could claim that we are of His created human race, therefore, as common children of God? When you break down the words used in this chapter, especially this verse, you will find from *Strong's Concordance* the Greek word for "name" here is *onoma*, which means authority, character, surname. It is from two root words: *ginosko*, which means to know, have knowledge of, understand, be aware of, and *oninemi*, which means "to receive profit or advantage, be helped (to have joy)." One other important word to know is the word for "in." As used here, it means "for the sake of, outwardly, as one." What does that imply? **Jesus is saying that He came outwardly, in the same authority, having the same character, as God the Father, so that we could be aware of, gain knowledge of, and understand God the Father's true character.** This is extremely bold!

Jesus's opening statement to the Pharisees got even more interesting as it went on. Pandora's box had been opened, and a very deliberate and statically charged dialogue began. I'm sure this raised the hair on the back of the Pharisees' neck. The axis of theological rotation was about to be catastrophically altered! There's no more guessing at who Jesus claimed to be after the exchange we're about to review in the Scripture here!

> **I and the Father are one.** (John 10:30 NASB)

Was He referring to being one in purpose with God or that Jesus and God were one and the same, or both?

> **And Jesus cried out and said, "He who believes in Me, does not believe in Me, but in Him who sent Me.**
> **And he that beholds Me beholds the One who sent Me."** (John 12:44–45 NASB)

> **If ye had known Me, you would have known My Father also: from now on you know Him, and have seen Him.** (John 14:7 NASB)

> **Jesus said to him, "Have I been so long with you, and yet you have not come to know Me, Philip? <u>He who has seen Me has seen the Father</u>; how do you say, 'Show us the Father'?"** (John 14:9 NASB; emphasis mine)

These verses clearly show that Jesus was saying that He was, in fact, God the Father. He is claiming to be God! That's bold! Not something you want to mess around with. If He's not God, and I'm standing next to Jesus when He is saying this, I might want to back away just a few feet! There's my old belief about God the Father's character coming out again. It gets even better.

Allow me to set the stage for this particular conversation. In John 8, the Pharisees had just brought the adulterous woman who was "caught in the very act" before Jesus to test Him. The Mosaic law says she should be stoned to death! Looking on the accused woman, who I'm fairly sure was guilty, Jesus calmly and quietly bends down and writes something on the ground. Can't know for sure what He wrote, but the Scripture twice mentions that the "finger of God" wrote something. The first one was the Ten Commandments. The second one was in the book of Daniel (chapter 5) when He wrote, "Mene, mene, tekel, upharsin," which means "God has numbered your kingdom and put an end to it. You have been weighed on the scales and found deficient. Your kingdom has been divided and given to the Medes and Persians." Jesus then said, **"He who is without sin among you, let him be the first throw a stone at her" (John 8:7).** He's implying in a subtle way that He is the "finger of God."

> **Then Jesus again spoke to them, saying, "I am the Light of the world; he who follows Me will not walk in the darkness, but will have the Light of life." (John 8:12** NASB)

The very next thing Jesus says after this encounter is written in John 8:12. The Pharisees and scribes were questioning the validity of who Jesus claimed to be. Jesus first replied that He was the "light of the world," and both the Father and Himself were credible witnesses to this fact. Okay then, He is claiming to be the light spoken of in Genesis 1, "And God said, 'Let there be light.'" He just possibly acted as though He was "the finger of God" and had them verify if they had met the sinless condition well enough to pass judgment on another (i.e., the adulterous woman). Then they questioned who His Father was. Jesus said they didn't know His Father and then made this reply.

> **And He was saying to them, "You are from below, I am from above: you are of this world, I am not of this world.**
> **Therefore I said to you, that you will die in your sins; for unless you believe that I Am (He), you will die in your sins."** (John 8:23–24 NASB)

Understand what Jesus is claiming here. The New Testament Scripture was originally written in Greek and Aramaic, not English. When it was translated to English, some words were added in the translation to make it easier reading for us. Those words are identified by *italicized* print in some versions and parentheses in others. Those words are not in the original text as inspired by God. Therefore, this passage as Jesus spoke it would be **"you shall die in your sins unless**

**you believe that I Am.**" Compare this with God's response to Moses when he asked God in **Exodus 3:14**, "Who should I say sent me?"

> **And God said to Moses, "I Am who i am,"**
> **and He said; "Thus you shall say to the sons**
> **of Israel, 'I Am has sent me to you.'" (Exodus**
> **3:14 NASB)**

The Pharisees immediately recognized that Jesus was claiming to be "Jehovah" here, and it really got them agitated. They immediately responded with "Who are you?" Jesus again attempted to explain it to them.

> **Jesus said, "When you lift up the Son of**
> **Man, then you will know that I Am *(He),* and**
> **I do nothing on My own initiative, but I speak**
> **these things as the Father taught Me." (John**
> **8:28 NASB)**

In an effort to save them from eternal death, Jesus left a future prophecy regarding His crucifixion on a cross in saying, "When the Son of Man be lifted up." This He might have said partly in hopes that when this event did in fact play itself out, they might remember Him speaking this phrase. He hoped that His claims of being the Messiah would draw them toward belief and lead them to salvation.

**John 8:30** says that many came to believe in Him. After Jesus encouraged those who had believed, the argumentative Pharisees continued. They were claiming superiority as God's chosen people due to the genealogical fact that Abraham was their father. Jesus attempted to explain to them that children imitate their father, and they were imitating the devil, not Abraham. Jesus attempted to help them understand that being God's chosen people was based on relationship with God (by faith), not on genealogy. Their hierarchy and political authority is being challenged, and they weren't amused. They liked the authoritative, elite position of wealth, power, and respect over the common class; and they weren't about to give it up!

These Jewish leaders became angry and accused Him of being demon possessed and asked Him, "Who do you make yourself out to be?" Jesus patiently again tried to draw them into trusting Him by giving them one last opportunity to understand.

> **"Your father Abraham rejoiced to see My day, and he saw *it*, and was glad."**
> **So the Jews said to Him, "You are not yet fifty years old, and have you seen Abraham?"**
> **Jesus said to them, "Truly, truly, I say to you, before Abraham was born, I AM." (John 8:56–58 NASB)**

This time He couldn't be any more direct. Then they just went "crazy"! This angered them so much that they immediately picked up stones to kill Him right there, but Jesus became hidden from their sight. Here, Jesus was surrounded by a mob of angry Pharisees and others in the temple area who had gathered around, and by some supernatural ability, they could not see Jesus. By the way, even the translators didn't attempt to add the extra word (*He*) here. Three times Jesus told them and all who read it today that He is the "I AM" in the burning bush that spoke to Moses and led him through the desert. Why three times? One for "I AM the Father," as referred to in the mention of Abraham; two for "I AM the Son," as He mentioned as coming "in the name (surname) of"; and three for "I AM the Holy Spirit," as referred to as being the One who spoke to Moses in the burning bush!

It became apparent through His exchange with the Jewish leaders that unless you were willing to believe that Jesus is YHWH, Jehovah, God the Father in human form, then you could not be saved from eternal spiritual death. It was of paramount importance! Here's why. Man is unable to save himself from death. No amount of good effort or good works will get us there. Even to sacrifice our own human blood as a redemptive substitute is not enough because our nature is corrupted by sin and uncleanness. Even human sacrificing in death to pay the death penalty for the sin of another isn't pure enough. God's standard of righteous purity is way too far above anything we could possibly offer. We were hopeless.

God had to send Himself in the form of Jesus Christ to willingly pay the death penalty with sinless blood on our behalf to make atonement for our hopelessly sinful condition. This is a pure act of selfless love for us. To reject God's own blood sacrifice as somehow not being good enough to redeem us and try to substitute in place of it any other religious combination of God's work plus obedience, or Jesus plus ritual/traditionalism, or any other form of religious idealism would be the highest insult a human could ever throw at God.

The Old Testament prophets knew of Jesus's coming and prophesied of it throughout the Scripture. One such example that supports the idea that Jesus is God is in **Micah 5:2** (NASB).

> **But as for you, Bethlehem Ephrathah, *Too* little to be among the clans of Judah, From you One will go forth for Me to be ruler in Israel. His goings forth are from long ago, From the days of eternity.**

I once had two members from the Jehovah's Witnesses Organization come to my house to visit about my salvation. After a very pleasant conversation and agreement on many common moral beliefs, we then split wide apart on how a man was saved from eternal spiritual death. I presented my view as outlined in this book. They disagreed, as the traditional Jehovah's Witnesses don't believe Jesus is God! They believe He is the son of God, but not God! In fact, they believe we are all "sons" of God. This was a critical error that carries with it an eternal spiritual death sentence! I took them to this verse in their own Bible and asked them to explain it.

This verse speaks of one who will be ruler of Israel that was born in Bethlehem (Ephrathah) and has lived eternally. Eternity has no beginning and no end. Jesus was born in Bethlehem. It is very clear that this verse spoke about Jesus, which they admitted. However, it also mentions He had no beginning and no end. They couldn't explain it. They graciously excused themselves and said they would consult with their superior on the matter and return. I tried to get them to set up a time for them to return. They wouldn't but said they would contact me. To my knowledge, they never called or came back. This issue is not negotiable. All roads don't lead to God. Some lead right into the pit of eternal separation from God!

So He is the "Light of the World." Jesus is also referred to as the Creator in many different places: **1 Corinthians 8:6, Hebrews 1:1–3, and Colossians 1:16**. In **John 1:1–4, 14** (NASB), the Scripture records who Jesus is and where He came from.

> **In the beginning was the Word, and the Word was with God, and the Word was God.**
> **He was in the beginning with God.**
> **All things came into being through Him, and apart from Him nothing came into being that has come into being.**
> **In Him was life, and the life was the Light of men...**
> **And the Word became flesh and dwelt among us, and we beheld His glory, glory as of the only begotten from the Father, full of grace and truth.**

I have presented this and even more evidence and to others in debate sessions but have still found some who will not believe. One particular person I remember counseling with, he was currently in prison and had been most of his teen and adult years. He wanted to change his life and had been trying to change by practicing different religions for quite some time. He had an incredible knowledge of the Scriptures, as much as some pastors I have met. However, for some reason, he was not able to experience behavioral change. As I sought the Spirit's guidance in understanding why there had been no change in his life, the Spirit led me to get his response to this evidence we have reviewed here in this chapter. He would absolutely not accept the truth that Jesus is God! Because of this, there was no power given. He was not saved, at least at that time. Maybe God used the visit as an opportunity to plant the seed, and I'll see him in the new heaven and earth.

Only God can give enough light in our hearts to see the truth of this. There are three passages that clearly state this the best: **1 Corinthians 2:10–14, 2 Corinthians 4:4,** and **John 6:64–65.**

> **But to us God revealed *them* through the Spirit, for the Spirit searches all things, even the depths of God.**
>
> **For who among men knows the *thoughts* of a man, except the spirit of the man, which is in him? Even so the *thoughts* of God no one knows, except the Spirit of God.**
>
> **Now we received, not the spirit of the world, but the Spirit who is from God, so that we may know the things freely given to us by God, which things also we speak, not in words taught by human wisdom, but in those taught by the Spirit, combining spiritual *thoughts* with spiritual *words.***
>
> **But a natural man does not accept the things of the Spirit of God, for they are foolishness to him; and he cannot understand them, because they are spiritually appraised. (1 Corinthians 2:10–14 NASB)**

This passage essentially says that an unbeliever cannot understand the written Word of God. Only the Spirit of God that has been put into the believing man's soul can reveal to the human mind the ability to understand the real meaning (thoughts) in God's written Word.

> **In whose case the god [Satan] of this world has blinded the minds of unbelieving, so that they might not see the light of the gos-**

**pel of the glory of Christ, who is the image of
God. (2 Corinthians 4:4 NASB)**

The word "image" in this verse means the exact representation. Also found in **Hebrews 1:1–3**.

**"But there are some of you who do not believe." For Jesus knew from the beginning who they were who did not believe, and who it was that would betray Him.**

**And He was saying, "For this reason I have said to you, that no one can come unto Me, unless it has been granted him from the Father." (John 6:64–65 NASB)**

Jesus is the same YHWH, Jehovah, Almighty God, Creator of all the universe that Noah, King David, priests, and all the other prophets prayed to. Make no mistake, without believing that Jesus is God Himself in the flesh, you would be an unbeliever, doomed to die in your sins. This is the main reason why some cannot understand the relationship of God the Father, Jesus the Son, and the Holy Spirit. It is because they choose not to. Unbelief! The patriarchs of the Old Testament looked forward to the coming Messiah who would redeem them from the hopeless sin condition and eternal death. Post Christ's crucifixion and resurrection believers look back at Christ our redeemer. The evidence has been presented, yet the choice of belief or unbelief still remains yours to make. It is truly by God's work of drawing and empowering us that we are able to trust by faith in His Truth.

The other main reason we needed to cover this issue is God has revealed Himself to man in different ways as man was able to grasp it. Over time, man has developed a corrupt idea of God's character. Therefore, Jesus came to reveal to us God the Father's true character in addition to providing the sacrificial Lamb (death penalty for sin) offering to save us. He came to give us a living, real, fleshly life as a human being, an example of what a real father's character was supposed to be like, rather than the corrupted idea we have had that has been passed on to us by our earthly fathers and father role models.

God is not limited to being at one place at one time as we are. We have a tendency to believe that God is confined to the same laws of nature that we are. God made the laws of nature. If you researched the vastness of the universe, you could begin to understand how absurd it is to believe that God could be contained solely in any space or form. God can be and is God the Father, Jesus the Son, and the Holy Spirit all at once yet is One God.

Jesus prayed to Himself as an example to us, to reveal to us the design for fellowship with our Creator that enables us to experience His life-transforming power. He is our example for life. He came to show us the way. He was also our example in submitting to baptism, even though He was without sin. He, by example, submitted Himself to come as a humble bond servant to reveal His character to us and urge us to take on the very same nature, humble and loving.

I still pray for that prison inmate as I think about him. I hope that one day the truth seed I planted will germinate and I will one day see him in heaven. If you are already a believer in Christ as God, carry this truth with you. Memorize it, and be equipped to boldly speak the truth to an unbelieving, deceived generation around you. What a joyful day we will have when we enter into His presence and see the ones we planted the seeds with, then give glory to God the Father who watered it and grew it, to save so many of us. We are His much-loved creation.

# THE SALVATION OF MOSES

WAS MOSES A "FOLLOWER" OF YHWH when he witnessed the burning bush or just familiar with the Hebrew legends about YHWH? I alluded to this question in chapter 2. During the exchange of conversation between God and Moses, Moses had to ask God, "Who should I say sent me?" It seemed that he didn't already know or maybe that he needed proof that it was the same God the Hebrews worshipped. Either way, from the appearance of asking this question, does the evidence support that Moses already had a practicing relationship with the God of the Hebrew faith? My belief is that he did not. If I am to make that assumption, I need to be able to provide some proof to support it. The subject discussed in this chapter provides that evidence.

Sometimes the Scripture records what appears to be contradictions in events recorded in multiple places throughout the sixty-six books of the Bible. I'm not foolish enough to claim there is a logical explanation for all of them. However, I believe there are explainable reasons for most of them. It's also known that new information becomes available later that sheds light on what was previously believed to be an error in the Scripture. This has been common as new archaeological evidence is constantly being unearthed.

It's also very likely that as over forty different authors wrote about God or historical events in the Holy Scriptures, they would've written it from their perspective or their limited viewpoint. They would be looking at the events through their own colored glasses, so to speak, as any of us would. God is still in control and able to keep the Scriptures holy and accurate. He cannot violate His own nature. Because all humanity is created "in His image" with the right of free choice, God cannot take away this free choice, even if directing fallen man to write the Scripture inspired by Himself! He is fully able to manage man's fallen condition, knowing there are going to be issues with it as mere men write the inspired Word of God. He's not worried about it and certainly has the power to correct these misconceptions somewhere later in the Scripture, without diluting theological accuracy, even if it required a different book and/or author of the complied Scriptures to correct the issue.

An example of this was previously mentioned with the account of David taking a census of the people in 2 Samuel 24:1 and 1 Chronicles 21:1. Here, the "anger of the Lord" and "Satan" were interchanged. I've found others as well, such as the seemingly benign or nonjudgmental account of Balaam in the Old Testament, however made clear his sin as written about him in Jude. There are many, and this book is not attempting to explain all those away in this writing, but in keeping with the theme of this book, it needed to be mentioned here as we come across some of those apparent contradictions. We will be required to reference back to this application again in the upcoming chapters. That said, allow me to pick up where we left off in the last chapter.

As discussed in chapter 3, God had sworn in **Isaiah 54:9** that He would not be angry with His people since the flood. Therefore, my belief is that God wasn't angry with Moses in **Exodus 4:14**; but Moses, the author of the book of Exodus, believed in his heart God was angry with him. He had a healthy fear of God but also was unable or reluctant to trust God. In the course of the discussion of this passage in a Bible study class, one of the participating members then asked, "Well, what about when God sought to kill Moses in **Exodus 4:24**, and his wife, Zipporah, circumcised his sons?" I wanted to skip this passage for obvious uncomfortable reasons, but after praying and studying it in detail, I realized that God was speaking through this class member. It cannot be overlooked.

**Then the anger of the Lord burned against Moses, and He said, "Is there not your brother Aaron the Levite? I know that he speaks fluently. And moreover, behold, he is coming out**

**to meet you; when he sees you, he will be glad in his heart.**

**You are to speak to him and put the words in his mouth; and I, even I, will be with your mouth and his mouth, and I will teach you what you are to do.**

**Moreover, he shall speak for you to the people; and he will be as a mouth for you and you will be as God to him. (Exodus 4:14–16 NASB)**

God's all-knowing and compassionate nature understood Moses's fear and apprehension. So what needs to be mentioned here is that God didn't just toss Moses aside and pick someone else for the chosen task. He designed Moses from birth and had been grooming his character to be the exact person for this chosen work. He also wanted to continue building the relationship with Moses, repairing the wounded heart he possessed due to life's painful events. God is inclined toward us the same way. What loving father wouldn't do the same for their own son? Are humans more loving, patient, and compassionate than God Himself?

God the Father, being understanding of Moses's fears and feelings of inadequacy, provided assistance in sending Aaron, Moses's brother, to speak on Moses's behalf. However, God made it clear that it would be Moses that He would speak and act through, not Aaron! Then God presented the staff to Moses from which He would perform the miracles through Moses. This could be thought of as both a security blanket and a reminder to Moses of His constant presence and power.

"You shall take in your hand this staff, with which you shall perform the signs."

Then Moses departed and returned to Jethro his father-in-law and said to him, "Please, let me go, that I may return to my brethren who

are in Egypt, and see if they are still alive." And
Jethro said to Moses, "Go in peace."

Now the Lord said to Moses in Midian, "Go
back to Egypt, for all the men who were seeking
your life are dead."

So Moses took his wife and his sons and
mounted them on a donkey, and returned to the
land of Egypt. Moses also took the staff of God
in his hand. (Exodus 4:17–20 NASB)

Notice that Moses took his wife and children with him back to
Egypt along with the "staff of God" firmly in his hand. Moses's first
step of obedience was to return to his family and father-in-law and
ask permission to return to Egypt to seek out the well-being of the
Israelites. Moses was also showing respect to his father-in-law and
other family members, knowing that his choices would affect not
only his own life, but the lives of the immediate family as well.

I believe many of us in our culture today make decisions based
only on what we want, thinking ourselves to be the center of the
universe and being inconsiderate of how these decisions might affect
the others around us. How we handle making decisions is passed on
to our children. If we make decisions that only consider our own
selfish interests and not the others around us, then our children,
who observe how we live, will more than likely begin making decisions based only on their own desires. Parents will most likely suffer the consequences of their own raising as the child grows older.
Conversely, being considerate of others in a selfless way is also passed
on to our children.

**The Lord said to Moses, "When you go
back to Egypt see that you perform before
Pharaoh all the wonders which I have put in
your power; but I will harden his heart so that
he will not let the people go.**

**Then you shall say to Pharaoh, 'Thus says
the Lord, "Israel is My son, My firstborn.**

> So I said to you, 'Let My son go that he may serve Me'; but you have refused to let him go. Behold, I will kill your son, your firstborn.'
>
> Now it came about at the lodging place on the way that the Lord met him and sought to put him to death.
>
> Then Zipporah took a flint and cut off her son's foreskin and threw it at Moses' feet, and she said, "You are indeed a bridegroom of blood to me."
>
> So He let him alone. At that time she said, "You are a bridegroom of blood"—because of the circumcision. (Exodus 4:21–26 NASB)

This exchange between God and Moses seems very out of character for a loving and just God. He appears very harsh and cruel when we look at what He told Moses to tell the Pharaoh (**verses 22 and 23**). Then Moses wrote in **Exodus 4:24** that He sought to kill Moses. God also tells Moses to perform all the wonders before the Pharaoh that God had shown him through His power. But then He tells Moses that the Pharaoh would not listen in spite of the miracles, because God "will harden his heart." Why would God want to "harden" the Pharaoh's heart?

There are several pieces of very important information in this passage that give a complete explanation of these difficult questions. To grasp a deeper understanding of this exchange between God and Moses here, it is necessary to break down the information God presented and research throughout the Scripture the significance of certain terms used.

The first important piece of information is that Israel is God's "firstborn." The term "firstborn" is used several places in the Scripture and carries a great deal of significance. One such place is in the New Testament book of **Colossians**. Notice in the following passage how the term "firstborn" is used.

**For He rescued us from the domain of darkness, and transferred us to the kingdom of His beloved Son, in whom we have redemption, the forgiveness of sins.**

**He is the image of the invisible God, the firstborn of all creation.**

**For by Him all things were created, both in the heavens and on earth, visible and invisible, whether thrones or dominions or rulers or authorities—all things have been created through Him and for Him.**

**He is before all things, and in Him all things hold together.**

**He is also head of the body, the church; and He is the beginning, the firstborn from the dead, so that He Himself will come to have first place in everything.**

**For it was the Father's good pleasure for all the fullness to dwell in Him, and through Him to reconcile all things to Himself, having made peace through the blood of His cross; through Him, I say, whether things on earth or things in heaven.**

**And although you were formerly alienated and hostile in mind, engaged in evil deeds, yet He has now reconciled you in His fleshly body through death, in order to present you before Him holy and blameless and beyond reproach. (Colossians 1:13–22 NASB)**

This passage is closely tied to the meaning being communicated in **Exodus 4:21–26**. Looking closely at the descriptions that are applied to Jesus in this text in Colossians, all these verses, speaking of Christ, call Him the "image of the invisible God" and "the firstborn of all creation," and **verse 16** describes Him as "the Creator God."

Jesus is referred to as the "image of the invisible God." This is the "invisible God" in heaven above that no man has ever seen (**John 1:18**). The Greek word for "image" actually means *the exact representation of, an exact duplicate.* This same concept is spoken of in **Hebrews 1:3**. Speaking of Christ, it says that *Jesus* is "the exact representation of His [God's] nature." The **Hebrew** words used in both **Colossians 1:15** and **Hebrews 1:3** are very similar in application to the idea of Christ being in God's "image." The word in **Colossians** is a word that describes a mirror reflection, like the reflection of the sun on a calm body of water. The word in Hebrews refers to a tool used to engrave stone or metal. When the metal tool is struck against the object, it leaves the exact imprint of the image on the tool in the object struck. The two are in fact the exact copy of the other. This is explicit to mean that Jesus is God in human form.

The third description of Jesus is that He is the Creator. He is the YHWH, Creator God of the universe: "all things were created by Him and for Him." This is also referred to in other passages such as **John 1:3**, **10**; **1 Corinthians 8:6;** and **Hebrews 1:2**. So this passage, when understood together, tells us that Jesus is the same invisible God of all the universe and the Creator of all that is. He was present with us in human form and is presented as the "firstborn" of all God's chosen (as a human being) ones.

The second description given was that Jesus is the "firstborn of all creation." John also called Him the "only begotten from the Father," which also could be understood as the "firstborn" Son of God, since God had begotten only One Son. God then explained to Moses in **Exodus 4:22** this very important concept: "Israel is My firstborn son!" It's important to look at the significance of this statement YHWH makes to Moses. You have heard many times the phrase "let My people go," but in **Exodus 4:23**, the LORD God says when speaking of Israel, "Let My son go." The LORD instructed Moses to tell the Pharaoh to let his "firstborn" go. Because he would not, the LORD will kill your (Pharaoh's) firstborn.

When comparing this information in **Colossians** to the passage in **Exodus**, we have to ask this question, "Who is the firstborn of God, Christ or Israel?" The answer is both, which we will explain later in this chapter. For now, keep in mind that God spoke to Moses about Israel being His "firstborn" immediately before this next verse in which the LORD "sought to kill Moses."

Notice also that **Colossians 1:18** links together the idea that Christ is the "firstborn from the dead" to being the head of the body, the church. We know God's chosen ones are the church. We, the church, are also set free from death to live an eternal abundant life existence. We will be raised from the dead just as Christ arose from the dead. Death no longer has hold or power over us.

As we connect this information to the passage in **Exodus 4**, note that just as we, believers in Christ, are the church (the chosen ones), so is the nation of Israel. They are also God's chosen ones, God's firstborn. We are the firstborn of the gentile age; the Israelites are the firstborn (the chosen) of the prophetic age. Still, all are chosen ones saved from eternal death by trusting in God by faith.

**Hebrews 12:22–23** (NASB) describes the chosen as the "church of the firstborn."

> **But you have come to Mount Zion and to the city of the living God, the heavenly Jerusalem, and to myriads of angels, to the general assembly and church of the firstborn who are enrolled in heaven, and to God, the Judge of all, and to the spirits of the righteous made perfect. (emphasis mine)**

The next important concept that we must understand from this passage in **Colossians** is how we were saved from death. **How were we selected to membership of being God's firstborn from death in this gentile age?** When reading again the passage in **Colossians 1,** the idea of reconciliation is the focus. Consider deeply the idea of being reconciled and brought into peace with God, forgiveness, and redemption.

The entire passage from Exodus 4:21–26 must be reviewed together to understand what the Scripture was trying to communicate. Upon first reading of this in **verse 24,** it appears to say that the LORD sought to kill Moses. As I mentioned earlier, this seems so out of character for God the Father. If taken out of context of the Scripture as a whole and understood only from the perspective of the English translation without reviewing the original Hebrew, it can very easily be misunderstood. I will attempt to explain how this verse can be written as truth yet maintain God's character of love.

Immediately following this verse, we read about Moses's wife, Zipporah, circumcising their children as a direct result of the "LORD seeking to kill Moses." Therefore, this circumcision appeased the LORD and "He let him [Moses] alone" **(verse 26)**. So it is necessary for us to research the significance of circumcision to give us an understanding of God's character as it applies in this passage. This act of circumcision was so powerful that it soothed God to the point of relenting from "seeking to kill Moses." The silver thread of truth regarding the "covenant of circumcision" throughout the Scripture reveals a great deal about God's perfect and righteous character.

> **This is My covenant, which you shall keep, between Me and you and your descendants after you: every male among you shall be circumcised.**
>
> **And you shall be circumcised in the flesh of your foreskin, and it shall be the sign of the covenant between Me and you.**
>
> **And every male among you who is eight days old shall be circumcised throughout your generations, a servant who is born in the house or who is bought with money from any foreigner, who is not of your descendants.**
>
> **A servant who is born in your house or who is bought with your money shall surely be circumcised; thus shall My covenant be in your flesh for an everlasting covenant.**
>
> **But an uncircumcised male who is not circumcised in the flesh of his foreskin, that per-**

**son shall be cut off from his people; he has bro-
ken My covenant." (Genesis 17:10–14 NASB)**

The first place in the Scripture that circumcision is mentioned
is **Genesis 17:10–14**. God has established a covenant between
Abraham and his descendants and Himself. Abraham's part of the
covenant was to **"walk before Me [God Almighty] and be blameless" (Genesis 17:1).** This word for "blameless" means "to be *whole,
without blemish, complete, full, perfect, without spot, undefiled.*"

I'm sure Abraham was thinking, *No sweat.* Being totally perfect,
unblemished, without spot, would be a cakewalk. Not! If you are
tuned into the reality of human nature, you realize God was asking
"Abe" to do the impossible! In any case, that was his part of the covenant. God's part was to multiply Abraham's seed into many nations,
make them fruitful, bring kings from his lineage, and give them the
land of Canaan (the land flowing with milk and honey). In other
words, God was giving him and his descendants the most fruitful
complete life possible on this earth.

Remember, the discussion here is who is included into membership of "God's chosen firstborn." This covenant was also to be
an "everlasting covenant" (**Genesis 17:7**), without end, eternal! This
was not only in respect to future generations observing this covenant,
but also God giving us insight that we will have life "everlasting," not
just life here on this earth. God's "chosen firstborn" have quality life
today, here on this earth (Canaan), as well as "everlasting" life without
end! This is a membership we definitely do not want to miss out on!

God said one more important thing, that He "will be their
God!" Then God commanded Abraham to circumcise every male
of at least eight days old or older. This circumcision was a sign or
seal that the covenant was received or accepted. The covenant was
not only offered to Abraham's descendants, but also extended to
all servants and foreigners who were bought and paid for and thus
included in Abraham's household. The condition of being covered by
the covenant was circumcision, and oh yeah, "Walk before Me [God
Almighty] and be blameless" (Genesis 17:1). One small part, the "be

blameless" part. If any person would not be circumcised, then that person would be "cut off" from his people.

So what did the act of circumcision signify? It was not an outward ritual that if you obeyed you were guaranteed full, quality eternal life. What about Abraham's part of the covenant? We can't just disregard his part of the deal—to be perfect! Another question that must be asked is "Who are of Abraham's household?" Always remember that the Scripture is the best interpreter of itself. So let's evaluate what God has told us about circumcision.

Before looking at the spiritual implications of circumcision, let's look at the physical application. The foreskin of the male penis would be difficult to keep clean because of the fold of skin. Often bacteria would be harbored and cause infections. These high bacterial infestations, which were on the outside of the skin on males, could be passed to the female during sex, thus causing the female to be susceptible to internal infections. These could in turn be passed on to the fetus. The child could suffer from a myriad of problems, including death! The cutting away of this fold of skin would prevent this problem.

If you remember, it was commanded to Abraham by God that this ritual be performed on the eighth day after a child's birth. Recent scientific studies have shown that the eighth day of the infant's life is the safest time to perform this procedure. This is due to the finding that vitamin K, which causes blood to coagulate, is not produced in sufficient amounts in the infant until the fifth through seventh day. On the eighth day, the body contains 10 percent more prothrombin than normal; prothrombin is also important in the clotting of blood. Cuts prior to the eight day or after the eight day would increase risk of excess bleeding in the infant. In that day, excessive bleeding could increase risk of weakness and infection.

What's more important to God is the spiritual condition of the human soul. So why such an emphasis on a physical health issue? If you keep following the silver thread of truth related to the subject of circumcision throughout the Scripture, you then find a passage in **Jeremiah 4:4** (NASB) that speaks to this idea.

> **Circumcise yourselves to the Lord and
> remove the foreskins of your heart, Men of
> Judah and inhabitants of Jerusalem, or else
> My wrath will go forth like fire and burn with
> none to quench it, because of the evil of your
> deeds.**

Here in this verse, God likened circumcision to a condition of
the heart. Here referring to an additional layer of flesh that keeps
the heart from being sensitive, feeling, and most of all, clean! This
extra calloused layer of skin is what we will refer to as "flesh." **First
Samuel 16:7** says that "man looks on the outward appearance, but
God looks on the heart." So even though the physical application
of circumcision is important, the spiritual application is greater. In
addition, this verse tells us that without circumcision of the heart,
God's unquenchable wrath will consume the person. Uncircumcised
in heart is also associated with evil deeds.

> **"Behold, the days are coming," declares
> the Lord, "that I will punish all who are cir-
> cumcised and yet uncircumcised—**
> **Egypt and Judah, and Edom and the sons
> of Ammon, and Moab and all those inhabit-
> ing the desert who clip the hair on their tem-
> ples; for all the nations are uncircumcised, and
> all the house of Israel are uncircumcised of
> heart." (Jeremiah 9:25–26 NASB)**

Here, the LORD makes clear that outward circumcision isn't
enough. The more important aspect of our relationship with Him is
the *circumcision of the heart*. Now look at what is said about the flesh
in the Scripture. The understanding becomes even more clear as we
follow the silver thread into the New Testament Word.

> **Now the deeds of the flesh are evident,
> which are: immorality, impurity, sensuality,**

> idolatry, sorcery, enmities, strife, jealousy, out-
> bursts of anger, disputes, dissensions, factions,
> envying, drunkenness, carousing, and things
> like these, of which I forewarn you, just as I
> have forewarned you, that those who practice
> such things will not inherit the kingdom of
> God. (Galatians 5:19–21 NASB)

Romans chapters 5 through 8 also describe for us that the flesh is the old nature of sin, which we used to live by to make decisions and find our identity. It is ruled by selfishness and is easily deceived. Living by the flesh results in pain, destruction, and ultimately death. The verses just prior to **Galatians 5:19–21** explain that outward circumcision has no effect on the spiritual relationship with God, but rather that only circumcision of the heart brings us into a right relationship with God. That those who rely upon the outward circumcision, as commanded by Abraham and Moses, could only achieve salvation from God if they were able to carry out perfectly the "whole law" (the "be perfect and blameless" part of the covenant) without even one flaw. This makes it clear that it was not the ritual of circumcision that provided salvation for mankind, but rather obedience to God's law, which is what the seal of circumcision represents—obedience! As both Abraham and Moses could attest to, this being perfect in performance to the "whole law" is impossible! Therefore, this idea of "circumcision of the heart" is the only hope for salvation for all humanity provided by God to receive the gift of eternal abundant life. So what is "circumcision of the heart"?

> You who boast in the Law, through your
> breaking the Law, do you dishonor God?
> For "the name of God is blasphemed
> among the Gentiles because of you," just as it
> is written.
> For indeed circumcision is of value if you
> practice the Law; but if you are a transgres-

**sor of the Law, your circumcision has become uncircumcision.**

**So if the uncircumcised man keeps the requirements of the Law, will not his uncircumcision be regarded as circumcision?**

**And he who is physically uncircumcised, if he keeps the Law, will he not judge you who though having the letter of the Law and circumcision are a transgressor of the Law?**

**For he is not a Jew who is one outwardly, nor is circumcision that which is outward in the flesh.**

**But he is a Jew who is one inwardly; and circumcision is that which is of the heart, by the Spirit, not by the letter; and his praise is not from men, but from God. (Roman 2:23–29 NASB)**

This passage in Romans reinforces that true salvation does not come from an outward ritual such as circumcision, but rather an inward condition of the heart. Circumcision of the heart! It is a cutting away of the "flesh" by which we as unbelievers formerly lived. In fact, Paul goes on to say that a Jew was not even a true Jew unless he has undergone a true circumcision of the heart. He also indicates in **verse 29** that "circumcision of the heart" is only accomplished by the **Spirit**. What does he mean here? Let's review two aspects of this truth.

In reality, Moses was living in an uncircumcision of the heart condition, outside of the Abrahamic covenant. **He was dead already!** He was raised in an Egyptian household being taught the Egyptian culture, including its form of worship to different gods. His children were born from a marriage to Zipporah, daughter of Jethro (who was the priest of Midian). They were raised in a pagan society. We don't know how old Moses's sons were, but they could be as old as thirty-nine years old, because this is forty years after he fled Egypt. They were still uncircumcised. <u>**Up to this point, Moses was raising his family without regard to the customs and practice of worship**</u>

**to the God of the Hebrews, YHWH.** It's obvious from the Scripture that Moses's children were uncircumcised, again outside of the protection of the Abrahamic covenant. Again, <u>they were dead already!</u>

So what about the "be perfect, blameless" part of total obedience to God without one mistake or flaw? That small thing was the real part of the covenant that had to be met by Abraham, Isaac, Jacob, Moses, of any and all of God's "chosen firstborn," which include gentile "believers in Christ" as well. Our only hope was spelled out clearly in the book of Romans, as written about in chapter 4. The silver thread of truth related to the subject of "circumcision" is continued.

> **Just as David also speaks of the blessing on the man to whom God credits righteousness apart from works:**
>
> **"Blessed are those whose lawless deeds have been forgiven,**
>
> **And whose sins have been covered.**
>
> **"Blessed is the man whose sin the Lord will not take into account."**
>
> **Is this blessing then on the circumcised, or on the uncircumcised also? For we say, "Faith was credited to Abraham as righteousness."**
>
> **How then was it credited? While he was circumcised, or uncircumcised? Not while circumcised, but while uncircumcised;**
>
> **and he received the sign of circumcision, a seal of the righteousness of the faith which he had while uncircumcised, so that he might be the father of all who believe without being circumcised, that righteousness might be credited to them, and the father of circumcision to those who not only are of the circumcision, but who also follow in the steps of the faith of our father Abraham which he had while uncircumcised.**

> **For the promise to Abraham or to his descendants that he would be heir of the world was not through the Law, but through the righteousness of faith.**
>
> **For if those who are of the Law are heirs, faith is made void and the promise is nullified; for the Law brings about wrath, but where there is no law, there also is no violation.**
>
> **For this reason it is by faith, in order that it may be in accordance with grace, so that the promise will be guaranteed to all the descendants, not only to those who are of the Law, but also to those who are of the faith of Abraham, who is the father of us all, (as it is written, "A father of many nations have I made you") in the presence of Him whom he believed, even God, who gives life to the dead and calls into being that which does not exist. (Romans 4:6–17 NASB)**

This passage makes it clear that it was because Abraham **believed** God by faith that he was considered righteous before God. And all who also believe God are considered Abraham's offspring. Salvation has always been determined by "faith" (putting your trust in a God you can't see), not by genealogy, denomination, or any other form of religion. Faith is an action word. This is where many people, if not all (and I include believers in Christ here as well as unbelievers), get totally off track. There is a tendency in religion to compare one's own behavior with another person's ability to carry out the law and/or live as a "good" person. Newer believers will get excited about their "new life" in Christ, pour into reading, memorizing the Word, and changing behavior patterns, which is what is supposed to happen as God's sanctifying goodness is at work in us. But then pride, conceit, and legalism creep in; and we get a bad case of the "Pharisees" disease. We can become what's described in Matthew 23:15, as Jesus spoke about the Pharisees, their proselytes becoming "twice the son of hell" as they were!

As believers mature, we put less and less emphasis on our ability to be righteous, and more and more thankfulness, with tears, in His grace! That's why when the woman was caught in the very act of adultery in John 8:3, the oldest accuser walked away first when Jesus said, "He who is without sin, cast the first stone." God's character and nature, His total essence and existence, is so holy and so pure that even the most microscopic speck of impurity or sin deems us incapable of existence with Him! **Please don't forget this. It's not a small matter. We have no hope of life or existence with such a Holy God without what our loving God did through Christ!** The righteous bar set for the god most people serve is way too low. We can't fathom His holiness, purity, and righteousness.

At this point, let me mention that there are two different covenants mentioned in the Scripture: the "covenant of Abraham" and that of the "law of Moses." The covenant of Abraham is an eternal covenant of "faith." The covenant of the law of Moses was a short-term covenant that was fulfilled when Christ became the sacrificial Lamb. Those who would attempt to obtain salvation by obedience to the "law of Moses" covenant, without the redemptive work of Christ, remain under the curse of keeping the law perfectly. The penalty even for one blemish is death! I would highly recommend against clinging to that method to get into God's good grace.

For those who are "in Christ," we have salvation through the "Abrahamic covenant" by "faith"! In this covenant, Christ paid the death penalty for our sin in full. The proof that your faith is real (active) is by your obedience to everything God is teaching through His Word and being empowered by His Spirit. This enables us to have a relationship with Him. In other words, we trust by faith that God made our salvation secure by the shed blood of Jesus on our behalf, paying our death penalty in full for all sin for us.

The second aspect we are to consider is "How is this accomplished by the Spirit?" Obedience only becomes possible through the indwelling Spirit of God that is given when we lay down our own control of our life and ask Him to indwell and give us new life. We become a new creation (**2 Corinthians 5:17; Galatians 2:20**).

> **For neither is circumcision anything, nor uncircumcision, but a new creation. (Galatians 6:15 NASB)**

> **For we are the true circumcision, who worship in the Spirit of God and glory in Christ Jesus and put no confidence in the flesh. (Philippians 3:3 NASB)**

In all the biblical examples it was clear that someone other than the one being circumcised had to perform the physical procedure. In other words, we are incapable of performing the circumcision of the heart on ourselves. It takes one who knows both our human spirit and God's Spirit. That would be none other than the Creator Himself.

> **And in Him you were also circumcised with a circumcision made without hands, in the removal of the body of the flesh by the circumcision of Christ;**
> **having been buried with Him in baptism, in which you were also raised up with Him through faith in the working of God, who raised Him from the dead. (Colossians 2:11– 12 NASB)**

> **For I say that Christ has become a servant to the circumcision on behalf of the truth of God to confirm the promises given to the fathers. (Romans 15:8 NASB)**

These passages make it clear not only that Christ performed our circumcision of the heart, but that <u>He did it by **being the circumci-**</u>

**sion**! The word "circumcision" means "to be cut off." He was cut off from the land of the living in order to make atonement for our sin. **He is our circumcision!**

> **He made Him who knew no sin to be sin on our behalf, so that we might become the righteousness of God in Him. (2 Corinthians 5:21 NASB)**

We now have life in that our death penalty for sin has been paid in full. Now remember that all foreign servants of Abraham's and Moses's households had to be bought with compensation before being eligible for circumcision, thus making them part of the household that was promised full abundant life. We too, in Christ, have been bought and paid for by Christ's blood, the bridegroom of the church.

> **For you have been bought with a price: therefore glorify God in your body. (1 Corinthians 6:20 NASB)**

Christ, our bridegroom, was the "bridegroom of blood." Moses was referred by his wife as being a "bridegroom of blood" to her. Now with this information, let's see if we can fully understand what was being communicated to Moses in this difficult passage in **Exodus 4:22–26**.

To understand the prophetic application of this passage in **Exodus 4**, you need to know that the name "Egypt" means "darkness, blackness; [deception] place of darkness, blackness; oppressors." Physically speaking, it was the place that God's chosen (His sons) are set free from. Spiritually speaking, this is the flesh condition from which believers (His sons, "chosen firstborn") are set free from in Christ today.

Moses as well as the Hebrew people were being saved from that "domain of darkness" mentioned in **Colossians 1:13**, which was Egypt. Set free from the rule and oppression of the Egyptians. Spiritually, all God's chosen are being freed from the "domain of darkness." That is, deception, being ruled by the evil deeds of the flesh, hostile in mind, and alienated from God **(verse 21)**. We are reconciled by the "circumcision of the heart" that can only be accomplished by Christ through His blood sacrifice. We receive the reconciliation and are transferred "to the kingdom of His beloved Son" by submitting our lives to obedience by faith (the Abrahamic covenant), which is empowered by the indwelling Spirit of Christ. Thus, we are considered "blameless, righteous" not by our own effort, but by that which is through Christ who is our "bridegroom of blood."

The LORD first explains to Moses that Israel is considered His firstborn son. And since the Pharaoh (god of darkness, evil) will not set His son (the chosen) free, the LORD will exchange the Pharaoh's firstborn son's life for His chosen people's life. In other words, death is the penalty for sin; and to be freed from the oppression of sin, a sacrifice of blood (someone's death) is required. Here, we can now understand that the Israelites are God's firstborn son in a physical sense. However, Jesus Christ is God's firstborn of the Spirit of God, the prototype of true believers today, those who are a "new creation" by the indwelling Spirit of God. Jesus "became sin" (darkness, blackness). This means he took on all the sin of all the chosen ones and died the sacrificial death—the blood death. The Pharaoh was considered by Egypt as a king, a god, a deity. The Pharaoh's son, the king (god) of Egypt's (darkness, blackness) son, is a representation and a foreshadowing of Jesus.

When Moses submitted to the Abrahamic covenant of obedience by faith, signified by the ordinance of circumcision, he accepted the prophesied Messiah as being the circumcision (being cut off), paying the death penalty, becoming the "bridegroom of blood," on his behalf, so his life was spared. Since he was already spiritually dead, this choice actually reconciled him to life.

Whether Moses clearly understood this concept fully or not is unknown, but what Moses did understand was that God was to be feared more than the Pharaoh and any gods the pagan nations worshipped! And to have life, he must be willing to submit to obedience to the One and Only Almighty God! God attempts to teach Moses several things by this event. First, what was it like to sacrifice a life so that another could live? Moses is facing death. Would Moses be willing to sacrifice his own life so that the people of Israel might live? Second, was Moses willing to die to himself and live by faith wherever God leads him and obey whatever God tells him? If so, then he would be required to observe the outward sign of allegiance to God, that being the circumcision of his household.

Moses knew about the ritual, but did his wife, Zipporah? It's unclear from the Scripture, but it appears to me that Moses told her what to do because she appeared to be disgusted with the idea as she threw the foreskins of the sons down at Moses's feet and said, "You are a bridegroom of blood to me." We do know, whatever she felt, that she submitted to the authority placed over her in obedience to circumcision of her family. Moses, by this act of circumcision, aligned himself and his family with the God of the Hebrews, YHWH. He committed himself to obedience to God. Thus, his life was spared.

Now, to reflect on the character of God the Father. **God's character of purity makes it impossible for Him to dwell with sin.** Therefore, all sin and those who are still subject to the penalty of sin will suffer God's unquenchable eternal destruction mentioned in **Jeremiah 4:4**. They are dead already.

There is a wrath of God. We may have difficulty understanding God's anger because the only type of anger we have ever witnessed is man's anger. Man's anger is corrupted due to emotions that are out of control due to a fallen condition from sin's influence. We automatically assume that God responds the same way man does when He is angry. God does not. One difference is that man's anger is driven by the motivation for vengeance. God's anger is driven by the motivation of love, an attempt to drive us back toward Him in submission that He might restore us to life. God was expressing to Moses, in love, that there is only one way to have life. It is in total commitment of our life to God. He will be our God, and we will be His people. After Moses's introduction to YHWH, God had to confirm before He went any further with Moses, "Are you Mine or not?" If not, death is the result. If you are His, life and the promises of the covenant are yours.

As we will study more about this later, we will find that when a life is taken, the Scripture often tells us that it is taken by the death angel, Satan. God is the giver of life, not the taker of it. However, God, who is in complete control over all that is, may allow death to occur if it is in compliance with His will. It is not God's will for evil to continue except for a short time, then it will be done away with—forever! God has made a plan to save His chosen (those who live by faith in Him) from death (eternal death). We can only be His chosen if we are willing to commit our lives to Him and accept that our death penalty for sin was paid for in full by Christ, our "bridegroom of blood." Our proof of being His chosen is "circumcision of the heart," the cutting away of being controlled by the flesh and being obedient to Him by the power of the indwelling Spirit. The choice to us today is still the same.

By the way, the word "sought" in **verse 4:24** means "to strive after, pursue, beg, ask, request require, seek." This indicates that God was striving after, asking, begging, pursuing, seeking for Moses to die to self and find life in obedience to God "by faith"! God is the life-giver. Moses chose life.

Before God could set His chosen people (the Israelites—His "firstborn") free from Egypt through Moses, He had to know if Moses was willing to submit to obedience by faith to God (which is the Abrahamic covenant). The act of circumcision was the seal or outward sign of submission to the covenant. Moses was already destined for God's eternal (unquenchable) wrath unless he was willing to submit his life to God in obedience.

I suspect by the fact that Zipporah performed the circumcision that Moses was very ill and couldn't perform the circumcision on his sons. Moses, who knew of the religious customs of the Hebrew people, instructed Zipporah to perform this seal of circumcision in order to save their lives, which, in essence, was true, as spiritually they were dead already.

The underlying messages of the Old Testament are always pointing to our salvation from eternal death by Christ's blood sacrifice to pay the penalty of our sin (darkness). He became our substitute "firstborn" of darkness as He became sin by paying the debt of sin on our behalf.

> **But thanks be to God that though you were slaves of sin, you became obedient from the heart to that form of teaching to which you were committed. (Romans 6:17 NASB)**

# God's Work, Not Moses's

Fear. It's what we fear most. The unknown and unpredictable outcome with the suspicion that something really bad can happen. Not for our good. It can paralyze us. And often does, into inaction, or avoidance. Sometimes that emotion is for our own good. It protects us from potential harm. The idea of jumping off a 150-foot cliff with nothing but rocks below, knowing the physics of gravity, keeps us from leaping. Adding a parachute or glider kite usually won't help that fear unless you've built up a little faith in those marvels of science to support you.

Moses finds himself in very much the same type of circumstances. In the conversation with God in the burning bush, he lost the "send someone else" argument over feeling inadequate. He now rises from the near-death experience with the Almighty God over the circumcision of his children, while his family is believing he's nuts. Through this, he realizes disobedience to God is a worse outcome than facing the fear of confronting the Pharaoh. Not to mention the idea of risking his life to become an advocate for the very slaves who rejected, disowned, and ridiculed him. Tough week for sure.

So Moses begins the process of confronting what was previously one of his greatest fears in life—going against the Pharaoh! Up against his army of soldiers, chariots, armed to the teeth, with nothing but a stick! No kidding, "a stick," better known as a "staff of God," as we'll expound on in the next few chapters. Oh, and of course, the Almighty God, but still… Even with whatever experience you've already had with God, pause a moment and consider what your emotions and thoughts would be here.

God begins the task of building that parachute of faith for Moses. He does this in several ways. First, He sends Aaron to be spokesman and "sidekick" for Moses. As previously mentioned, He provides some miracle support by using the "staff of God" (**Exodus 4**). Imagine that, a staff empowered by the Almighty God to help hold up his wobbly legs. And the miracle of restoring the leprous hand was to remind Moses that it wasn't his own hand that would accomplish the task of standing up to the Pharaoh to set the Israelites free, but the restored "hand of God" that would bring it about! Moses and Aaron gather the elders of Israel and pass on to them the words of the LORD. Those words were confirmed by the miracles Moses performed before them according to what God commanded. When the people saw the miracles and heard of God's compassion, they "worshipped."

> **And afterward Moses and Aaron came and said to Pharaoh, "Thus says the Lord, the God of Israel, 'Let My people go that they may celebrate a feast to Me in the wilderness.'"**
> **(Exodus 5:1 NASB)**

God sends Moses to the Pharaoh to ask permission to let the Hebrew slaves go so they can "celebrate a feast" to their God in the wilderness. Hmmm, okay, seems innocent and harmless enough. The Hebrews have now been in Egypt for four hundred years, most of it in captivity, providing most of all the heavy labor for the Egyptian Pharaohs' projects of building their monuments, tombs, sphinxes, temples, etc. I'm sure they need a vacation after all that anyway. The wilderness isn't too far, and I'm sure they'll want to be back for dinner. They'll be refreshed, happy, and ready to make another four-hundred-year run at the hot, heavy manual workload under those "nice" taskmasters. They'll be more productive after a nice day or so off. Why wouldn't the Pharaoh agree?

There's really another interesting thing about this request. It is the type of worship God was describing He wanted from the Israelites. The Hebrew word for "celebrate a feast" is *chagag*, which means to "dance, celebrate, reel to and fro, hold a feast (holiday), to be giddy." The second word in this passage that I would like to bring attention to is the word for "to Me." It is the prefix "le," which means "to, toward, for the purpose of, in (into), belonging to, with respect to." So when we look at the meanings of these two words together, I understand it to say, "Dance, celebrate, be giddy because you belong to Me and are created for the purpose of Me, and you are in Me."

This type of worship describes something I haven't seen in most of the traditional worship services I've been in most of my life. In fact, the services I witnessed as I was growing up were more like a funeral than this type of celebration described. In the churches I grew up in, one who exhibited this type of worship might have been excommunicated due to "wild and irreverent" behavior. If we truly knew the magnitude of what this type of worship really meant, our worship today wouldn't be so dry. It would be more of what God intended it to be.

> **God said to Abram, "Know for certain that your descendants will be strangers in a land that is not theirs, where they will be enslaved and oppressed four hundred years.**
> **But I will also judge the nation whom they will serve, and afterward they will come out with many possessions. (Genesis 15:13–14 NASB)**

In Genesis 15:13–14, God gave a specific prophecy about Abraham's descendants being enslaved and oppressed in a foreign land for four hundred years. That God would then judge the nation that oppressed them, set them free, and give them the oppressors' possessions! After four hundred years of hard and brutal treatment in the sunbaked Egyptian heat, do you think the Israelites would be in a state of believing freedom is at hand or more in a state of unbelief? Do you think they would feel like worshipping (to dance, reel to and fro, hold a feast, be giddy) their God in this way? Without faith, no! On the other hand, if they knew the promise God had already made to Abraham (**Genesis 15:13**) some six hundred years earlier, to set his descendants free after enduring this four hundred years of captivity and oppression by foreign power, then they might have a glimmer of hope. Negative emotions are very hard to overcome. Remember, they didn't have the written word from God, because Moses had not written the Pentateuch yet.

Those prophecies were passed down verbally from generation to generation about their God, even though they would know by the given timetable that this is now four hundred years later. Would they have faith in their God? His four-hundred-year silence and inaction would've quieted that faith down to a word mumbled under their breath. However, Moses had just seen and heard from the LORD, telling the people that God is now going to set them free. If they truly knew their God, and if they believed their God, then they would dance and leap with celebration knowing that it's about to happen! But did they? I very seriously doubt it. The truth is, with those circumstances, neither would we. The sad truth is we complain about difficult circumstances at work, which we get paid to do, then go home in our car with AC to a home with AC and veg out to the TV in our freedom—at least in modern America and many other affluent societies across the world.

**But Pharaoh said, "Who is the Lord that I should obey His voice to let Israel go? I do not know the Lord, and besides, I will not let Israel go." (Exodus 5:2 NASB)**

The stage is set for the ensuing conflict. The question is who or what is the conflict? The Pharaoh against Moses? The Pharaoh against the Israelites? God against the Pharaoh? The Pharaoh says, "I don't know this God of Israel. He's not my God; therefore, I don't care about your requests" (paraphrased). The Pharaoh worships a different god, namely himself! His basic position is that this God must be more powerful than I am to make me do what you request. God had already told Moses this would be the case. This is important to understand, as it will help us understand why God approached things in the way He did. This was more than just setting the captive free. It was also about displaying to the known world who **IS** the most powerful God of all gods. By the way, the Pharaoh suffered from the same deception that every human being suffers from, which is the belief that we are our own god!

> **They will pay heed to what you say; and you with the elders of Israel will come to the king of Egypt and you will say to him, "The Lord, the God of the Hebrews, has met with us. So now, please, let us go a three days' journey into the wilderness, that we may sacrifice to the Lord our God." Exodus 3:18**

> **Then they said, "The God of the Hebrews has met with us. Please, let us go a three days' journey into the wilderness that we may sacrifice to the Lord our God, otherwise He will fall upon us with pestilence or with the sword." (Exodus 5:3 NASB)**

Notice that Moses asked the Pharaoh to "please let us go." This was in direct obedience to the way God commanded Moses to speak to the Pharaoh in **Exodus 3:18**. God was teaching Moses (and us as well) that we should be respectful and kind to all, even men of evil, and respectful of their God-given right to choose. As long as people treat others with disrespect and speak forcefully or condescendingly, a favorable outcome will most likely not occur. You will reap resistance!

> **Or do you think lightly of the riches of His kindness and tolerance and patience, not knowing that the kindness of God leads you to repentance? (Romans 2:4 NASB)**

**Romans 2:4** tells us that **"it's the kindness of the LORD that leads us to repentance."** The Pharaoh probably perceived this show of respect as a weakness, as most people do today. But this New Testament verse seems in contrast to **Exodus 5:3** when they said of

God, **"Otherwise He will fall upon us with pestilence or with the sword."** How can these both be true? It's grace that brings about a changed heart in fallen man. God is trying to change the wounded hearts of both the Hebrew people and Moses, trying to restore their faith in Him to save them and restore life. It rarely looks the way we think it should.

I remember my stepdaughter going with a group on an evangelical mission trip. They had T-shirts printed with a slogan on the back: "TURN OR BURN!" While it may be true, knowing the resistant, rebellious heart of fallen man, I don't believe it will bring about an effective heart change. Forcing man into obedience breeds rebellion instead of a love relationship. It may bring a temporary desire to buy "fire insurance," but people will run from a God who punishes without love, instead of to Him. A "fire insurance" gospel will be devoid of love. Consequently, the leaders of those groups will be oppressive over the followers, filling them with all kinds of legalistic performance requirements. Real love will be absent.

What about the go and sacrifice to God "lest He fall on us with pestilence or (kill us) with the sword"? Really? Is that what God would do to His people? This is another one of those difficult passages that affects the way we view God. To truly understand this passage, we need to understand the character of God the Father. God's character of purity and perfection must always be remembered. His character of purity cannot be compromised. **Habakkuk 1:13** (NASB) tells us that God cannot look upon sin (evil). It will be destroyed.

> **Your eyes are too pure to approve evil, and You cannot look on wickedness with favor. Why do You look with favor on those who deal treacherously? Why are You silent when the wicked swallow up those more righteous than they?**

The only part of the fallen human race that will be spared are the people who have been freed from the penalty of death. This is only possible by accepting Christ's payment of paying the death penalty on your behalf. His intent is to redeem your life from death, a blood atonement to set you free. He died in your place. Accepting this payment comes with a price, which is a willingness to surrender ownership and control of your own life to a desire to become obedient to God.

The pestilence, or a plague (sickness, violence, pain), is the result of a life lived outside of God's design. Pestilence is what occurs first, which is designed to drive us back to God and His plan to save us from certain death. If anyone refuses God's provision of salvation, then eternal destruction is the only other alternative left. God's character of purity cannot be compromised. However, neither can God's character of love. Jesus Christ, the Lamb of God, **who is God**, sacrificed Himself to pay the death penalty on behalf of those who would die to being god of their own life and accept life in Him. Moses knew from the traditional Hebrew rituals of worship generationally passed down that worship of the Hebrew God required a blood (animal) sacrifice to atone for sin in man. Without it, plague would come first, death second. He had gained understanding of this concept firsthand through his experience with God over the circumcision issue.

God's methods of saving, rescuing, or restoring life to us often seem to be contrary to what we believe to be in our best interest, as we're about to see with Moses and the Israelites.

> **But the king of Egypt said to them, "Moses and Aaron, why do you draw the people away from their work? Get back to your labors!"**
>
> **Again Pharaoh said, "Look, the people of the land are now many, and you would have them cease from their labors!"**
>
> **So the same day Pharaoh commanded the taskmasters over the people and their foremen, saying,**
>
> **"You are no longer to give the people straw to make brick as previously; let them go and gather straw for themselves.**

But the quota of bricks which they were making previously, you shall impose on them; you are not to reduce any of it. Because they are lazy, therefore they cry out, 'Let us go and sacrifice to our God.'

Let the labor be heavier on the men, and let them work at it so that they will pay no attention to false words."

So the taskmasters of the people and their foremen went out and spoke to the people, saying, "Thus says Pharaoh, 'I am not going to give you any straw.

You go and get straw for yourselves wherever you can find it, but none of your labor will be reduced.'"

So the people scattered through all the land of Egypt to gather stubble for straw.

The taskmasters pressed them, saying, "Complete your work quota, your daily amount, just as when you had straw."

Moreover, the foremen of the sons of Israel, whom Pharaoh's taskmasters had set over them, were beaten and were asked, "Why have you not completed your required amount either yesterday or today in making brick as previously?"

Then the foremen of the sons of Israel came and cried out to Pharaoh, saying, "Why do you deal this way with your servants?

There is no straw given to your servants, yet they keep saying to us, 'Make bricks!' And behold, your servants are being beaten; but it is the fault of your own people."

But he said, "You are lazy, very lazy; therefore, you say, 'Let us go and sacrifice to the Lord.'

> **So go now and work; for you will be given
> no straw, yet you must deliver the quota of
> bricks." (Exodus 5:4–18 NASB)**

The Pharaoh's response was to increase the hard labor in a show of "who's boss!" Obviously, the Pharaoh did not know who he was dealing with. In a sense, he was drawing a line in the sand and daring the Almighty God, Creator of the universe, to cross over. He instructed the taskmasters to withhold straw to make bricks but require the same quota of production. This meant they would work longer and harder and were beaten in the process for failure to carry out the increased load. Actually, it was the "foremen" who were beaten for the failure of the workload success. These foremen were Hebrews who were forced to drive their own people in this slave labor. Notice what the foremen said to the Pharaoh in **Exodus 5:15–16** (NASB).

> **Then the foremen of the sons of Israel
> came and cried unto Pharaoh, saying, "Why
> do you deal this way with your servants?
> There is no straw given to your servants,
> yet they keep saying to us, 'Make bricks!' and
> behold, your servants are being beaten; but it's
> the fault of <u>your own people</u>." (emphasis mine)**

Here, there is a distinction between the Hebrew foremen and the taskmasters **(verse 5:6)** who were Egyptians. I'm sure the Pharaoh was feeling their pain as he said that they were "lazy." If they had time to party with their God, then there must not be enough work for them to do. I know bosses like this. Nothing new under the sun. Employees fear asking to take their Saturday or Sunday off in order to worship, for fear of losing their jobs.

> **The foremen of the sons of Israel saw that
> they were in trouble because they were told,
> "You must not reduce your daily amount of
> bricks."**

> **When they left Pharaoh's presence, they met Moses and Aaron as they were waiting for them.**
>
> **They said to them, "May the Lord look upon you and judge you, for you have made us odious in Pharaoh's sight and in the sight of his servants, to put a sword in their hand to kill us."**
>
> **Then Moses returned to the Lord and said, "O Lord, why have You brought harm to this people? Why did You ever send me?**
>
> **Ever since I came to Pharaoh to speak in Your name, he has done harm to this people, and You have not delivered Your people at all." (Exodus 5:19–23 NASB)**

The foremen could see many more beatings ahead as they knew the impossibility of the task, and the Pharaoh didn't feel their pain as they had hoped. So they went to what they thought was the source of their trouble, Moses and Aaron! Their main complaint was that they had caused them to become "odious" in the Pharaoh's sight. I got news for them—they were already considered "odious" in the Pharaoh's sight, because they were considered a second-class slave people. If I understand what I'm reading accurately, the foremen weren't necessarily concerned about the Hebrew people being "odious" to the Pharaoh. Their concern was that they (the foremen) were now being treated as regular slaves since they were being beaten along with the rest of the Hebrew population! Previously, they were considered as officers, rulers, and overseers. Isn't that like us today? The Christians being beaten and martyred in other countries don't really bother us until the oppression moves into our own backyard, affecting us!

> **Then Moses returned to the Lord and said, "O Lord, why have You brought harm to this people? Why did You ever send me?**

> **Ever since I came to Pharaoh to speak in Your name, he has done harm to this people, and You have not delivered Your people at all."**
> **(Exodus 5:22–23 NASB)**

Actually, Moses's response to God sounds like many of my own prayers. It's almost as if Moses was saying, "Lord, I don't think you know what You are doing. It's getting worse. See, I told you I wasn't the one for the job, and You haven't done what You said You would at all!" Here, it appears Moses believed everything was to go smoothly. When we pray for healing from an illness, lost job, or pending trouble, don't we think God ought to turn things around immediately? With methods and timing that we understand?

> **Then Moses said to the Lord, "Please, Lord, I have never been eloquent, neither recently nor in time past, nor since You have spoken to Your servant; for I am slow of speech and slow of tongue."**
> **The Lord said to him, "Who has made man's mouth? Or who makes him mute or deaf, or seeing or blind? Is it not I, the Lord?**
> **Now then go, and I, even I, will be with your mouth, and teach you what you are to say."**
> **But he said, "Please, Lord, now send the message by whomever You will."**
> **Then the anger of the Lord burned against Moses, and He said, "Is there not your brother Aaron the Levite? I know that he speaks fluently. And moreover, behold, he is coming out to meet you; when he sees you, he will be glad in his heart.**
> **You are to speak to him and put the words in his mouth; and I, even I, will be with your**

**mouth and his mouth, and I will teach you what you are to do.**

**Moreover, he shall speak for you to the people; and he will be as a mouth for you and you will be as God to him.**

**You shall take in your hand this staff, with which you shall perform the signs." (Exodus 4:10–17 NASB)**

Remember the exchange between God and Moses in **Exodus 4:10–17**. Moses again resorted to his low self-esteem as the cause of the problem. God was also trying to teach Moses that it was not his ability that was going to get the job done, but rather the power of God. How often do we keep telling God, "I can't do this or that ministry because of my lack of skill or training"? That excuse doesn't wash. It didn't work for Moses, and it doesn't work for us either.

My father was a pastor who was deeply committed to his work. I love my father as he taught me so much. Over the years, I remember him saying, "I was called into the ministry." Even after he resigned from ministry late in life, he still kept saying, "I was called." In his mind, that somehow made him feel resolve for the emotional pain he might have suffered from, creating a sense of worth and value to God. Pastors really do suffer a great deal because of the way people ostracize them. The reality is **"we are all called!"** In what ways are you allowing God to work through you to accomplish His plan for His kingdom right now?

Take notice of one other important point in the passage in **Exodus 5:22–23**. Moses kept referring to the people as "this people" and "Thy people." Moses, a fellow Hebrew, for whatever reason, is not at a place where he is willing to accept himself as being one of his own Hebrew people. He views himself differently than he views them. He is finding it difficult to identify with the people. Maybe he sees himself as more righteous than the people, maybe because they rejected him as one of their own when he was a younger man in Egypt, maybe because of the pain of his father putting him out to die in the river to avoid persecution by the Pharaoh. We could only speculate as to the reason, because there is not enough evidence at this point to know. I do believe this is additional evidence that Moses was wounded from childhood as discussed in chapter 1, contributing to his anger inside. It will surface again later, and I will address this point in more detail.

> **Then the LORD said unto Moses, "Now you shall see what I will do to Pharaoh: for by a strong hand shall he let them go, and by a strong hand shall he drive them out of his land.**
>
> **And God spake unto Moses, and said unto him, I am the LORD [YHWH]:**
>
> **and I appeared unto Abraham, unto Isaac, and unto Jacob, as God Almighty; but My name LORD [YHWH] I did not make Myself known to them. (Exodus 6:1–3 NASB)**

God's plans are more all-encompassing than just our own corner of the universe. He wants to do much greater things than our small minds can comprehend. Remember, the plagues are designed to drive us toward God in repentance that He may give us life. Believe it or not, God loved the Pharaoh and the Egyptians just as much as He did the Israelites. He wanted them all to know the power and great love of the only God of creation.

God was trying to tell Moses that He needed to allow the Pharaoh to show his full power so that God's power, by comparison, would put a proper perspective on things. In other words, "Now that you see what the Pharaoh 'thinks' he can do, let Me show you what I 'will do'!" He reminds Moses that He is the "I AM." He wants the whole world to know of His unmatched power.

There are two important points in this passage in **verse 3**. Look at it again closely. The first point is that God expresses Himself in a way that He had not done before. God informs Moses that He is the same God who dealt with Abraham, Isaac, and Jacob; but one difference was that God did not reveal His proper name to them as He had to Moses. His name is YHWH. This is an implication of God's tender, loving desire to have a close, intimate fellowship with Moses and all of His chosen ones. This would only be possible through the ordinance of the blood sacrifice, which He will institute through the ceremonial law given later by Moses. God also assured Moses that He would indeed free the people from bondage and bring them into the land of Canaan.

The second point is that God has been revealing Himself in stages throughout time. He first revealed Himself as the Almighty God to Abraham, Jacob, and Isaac. He now is revealing Himself as YHWH, Jehovah God. His intimate name. The name Jehovah means "God saves" or the "God who saves." Here, the Scripture supports the idea that God is unraveling His nature and character toward us throughout different periods and different leaders. Even though Moses saw Him as an angry, punishing God, God reveals His true character of mercy, grace, and love through the prophets who followed and ultimately through Jesus Christ Himself.

> **Then I will take you for My people, and I will be your God; and you shall know that I am the Lord your God, who brought you out from under the burdens of the Egyptians. (Exodus 6:7)**

God makes clear to Moses that one purpose in all these events is to rescue His people for a possession to fellowship with—in essence, to have a relationship with them. To love, bless, give freedom, and know Him. Another was to restore their faith in His ability to care for and protect them. A Father relationship.

> **So Moses spoke thus to the sons of Israel, but they did not listen to Moses on account of their despondency and cruel bondage. (Exodus 6:9)**

During a divorce, I remember going through an intense emotional struggle over the possibility of losing my children in court over custody. It wasn't just custody, but a fear of losing the relationship with them completely! It was excruciatingly painful. No matter what others who cared tried to say to console me, I would not and could not listen or find any hope in their words. The pain and fear overwhelmed me to the point of losing all rationale. It appears to me this may be a similar emotion the Israelites were experiencing. God rescued them in spite of their inability to have faith.

Our salvation works the same way. It is the work of God even to bring us to a place of trusting by faith. He builds the faith in us. None of it is our doing, but rather all of it is God's plan—His work and responsibility. Just the same as it is a father's responsibility to grow a child's understanding of life. A child has no experience to connect the dots. Nothing to draw from. Totally susceptible to deception. A father teaches, nurtures, protects, and creates the ability for a child to have faith in things the father teaches and provides (**1 Corinthians 1:18–2:5**, especially **verse 30**, and **2:5**).

> **For the word of the cross is foolishness to those who are perishing, but to us who are being saved it is the power of God.**
>
> **For it is written, "I will destroy the wisdom of the wise, and the cleverness of the clever I will set aside."**
>
> **Where is the wise man? Where is the scribe? Where is the debater of this age? Has not God made foolish the wisdom of the world?**
>
> **For since in the wisdom of God the world through its wisdom did not come to know God, God was well-pleased through the foolishness of the message preached to save those who believe.**
>
> **For indeed Jews ask for signs and Greeks search for wisdom;**
>
> **but we preach Christ crucified, to Jews a stumbling block and to Gentiles foolishness, but to those who are the called, both Jews and**

Greeks, Christ the power of God and the wisdom of God.

Because the foolishness of God is wiser than men, and the weakness of God is stronger than men.

For consider your calling, brethren, that there were not many wise according to the flesh, not many mighty, not many noble; but God has chosen the foolish things of the world to shame the wise, and God has chosen the weak things of the world to shame the things which are strong, and the base things of the world and the despised God has chosen, the things that are not, so that He may nullify the things that are, so that no man may boast before God.

But by His doing you are in Christ Jesus, who became to us wisdom from God, and righteousness and sanctification, and redemption, so that, just as it is written, "Let him who boasts, boast in the Lord."

Chapter 2

And when I came to you, brethren, I did not come with superiority of speech or of wisdom, proclaiming to you the testimony of God.

For I determined to know nothing among you except Jesus Christ, and Him crucified.

I was with you in weakness and in fear and in much trembling, and my message and my preaching were not in persuasive words of wisdom, but in demonstration of the Spirit and of power, so that your faith would not rest on the wisdom of men, but on the power of God. (Corinthians 1:18–2:5 NASB)

> **But Moses spoke before the Lord, saying, "Behold, the sons of Israel have not listened to me; how then will Pharaoh listen to me, for I am unskilled in speech?" (Exodus 6:12)**

> **But Moses said before the Lord, "Behold, I am unskilled in speech; how then will Pharaoh listen to me?" (Exodus 6:30)**

Moses is still trying to believe that his own ability (or inability) has something to do with God's plan to save the Israelite people. He is stuck, as he has repeated this several times **(Exodus 4:30, 6:12, 30)**. I believe we are the same way. The LORD was trying to teach Moses that neither the Israelites nor the Pharaoh was anything to be concerned with, but rather the power of God! God's only response in **verse 13** was "to bring the sons of Israel out of Egypt"! Isn't His charge to us the same? Trust Me and obey! He will do the work. Your low self-esteem, your past (and present) sins, and your inadequate abilities do not hinder God's ability to accomplish His intentions. How arrogant we would be to think in some way we have something to offer God that would be of any use other than our availability and obedience.

> **And I will harden Pharaoh's heart, that I may <u>multiply</u> My signs and My wonders in the land of Egypt. (Exodus 7:3; emphasis mine)**

God's purpose was made very clear to Moses. He wanted to show the sons of Israel His true power as God Almighty as well as His character of purity, tenderness, loving-kindness, and compassion toward His people. He wanted to reveal Himself in a more intimate way. He revealed for the first time His name, YHWH. One of the reasons He allowed the Pharaoh's heart to become more and more hardened was to increase His demonstration of ultimate, superior power. So not just Pharaoh, but Israel, all of Egypt, and the rest of the world throughout time would begin to take notice of this God of the Hebrews. God tried to reach both the Pharaoh and the Egyptian people. To save them.

The conflict was not Pharaoh against Moses, Pharaoh against the Israelites, or God against Pharaoh. It was God's love saving His created human race from self-destruction. He was saving us from our own fallen nature. The conflict was saving us from trying to be our own god. Another word for it today is "humanism"—the idea that we are capable of saving ourselves by human thinking and effort. It ends up in historical events like communism, socialism, elitism, etc., where mass euthanasia is used to solve things like the food shortage problem. Or killing off what is perceived to be a genetic flaw in a given race. Or killing anyone who disagrees with a given philosophy for the "greater good."

God also desires us to know His promises and trust in His faithfulness. Then we can be used by God to bring His kingdom about in other people's lives. In doing so, we will experience a joy that is unmatched by any other earthly experiences. Our worship will become more and more of a celebration as our faith in Him grows. Yield your life to Him in the work He has chosen for us so that we might also experience the miracles of God in our own lives.

It's not about us; it's never been about us. It's always been about Him. He is the One worthy of all adoration and praise. He does the work. His perfect plan will be accomplished without fail! Both in us and in this present universe. God loves and responds toward us as if it's always been about us. Just like we make our little children the center of attention in our world, He also makes us His center of His attention showing His great love for us. Just in case you're still believing that somehow our life, faith, and growth depend on our ability to perform, please read the following additional verses.

**That He would grant you, according to the riches of His glory, to be strengthened with power through His Spirit in the inner man. (Ephesians 3:16)**

Now to Him who is able to do far more abundantly beyond all that we ask or think, according to the power that works within us. (Ephesians 3:20)

For I am confident of this very thing, that He who began a good work in you will perfect it until the day of Christ Jesus. (Philippians 1:6)

For it is God who is at work in you, both to will and to work for His good pleasure. (Philippians 2:13)

I can do all things through Him who strengthens me. (Philippians 4:13)

For we are His workmanship, created in Christ Jesus for good works, which God prepared beforehand that we should walk in them. (Ephesians 2:10)

Abide in Me, and I in you. As the branch cannot bear fruit of itself unless it abides in the vine, so neither can you unless you abide in Me.
I am the vine, you are the branches; he who abides in Me and I in him, he bears much fruit, for apart from Me you can do nothing. (John 15:4–5)

It's God's work; trust Him and walk fearlessly and boldly in it.

# LIFE-GIVER OR DESTROYER?

HAVE YOU EVER HEARD THE phrase "The Lord giveth, and the Lord taketh away?" Do you believe God causes for destruction the powerful weather patterns like tornadoes, hurricanes, tsunamis, volcano eruptions, earthquakes, etc., commonly referred to as "acts of God"? Does God take life? The real question is "Are they true?" Most people would probably say yes to this question. Remember the Scripture is our source of truth. Therefore, to evaluate the validity of these phrases that shape our view of God's character, we must pass them through the filter of God's word to know if they really are true or another one of Satan's disguised lies. We also know Satan uses just enough truth in order to make the bigger lie more believable. For example, does the Lord give and take away? This ideology is presented in the Scripture in **Job 1:21, 9:12, and 27:8**. Yes, God is the Creator of all things, and ultimately all good things come from the Lord. He does impart the breath of life and soul into a human being, and He requires it back once life to the mortal body has ended. But is it God who actually takes the life from the person's mortal body?

How about the weather patterns, does God control the weather? Yes, of course, the Scripture gives us many accounts of God's control of not just calming the storms but also positions of the sun, darkness during the day, draught and flood, etc. But the other side of those truths must be analyzed in those phrases. Does God destroy by weather patterns? Does God take away life? Down through the ages, most people would believe He does; but what does God's word present, as a whole, of these questions? This book is not an exhaustive pursuit in answering all these difficult questions but will explore some of these more pointed ones that leave a lasting impression on our view of God's character and nature. This is extremely important, because what we believe about how God works in these events affects how we view God's character.

The Scripture does give us some insight to the character of both God the Father (especially through examination of Jesus's character displayed) and Satan. We know God the Father loved the created human race so much that He sacrificed Himself to an excruciatingly horrible death to save it. We'll examine more of God's character later in the chapter.

Allow me to first briefly identify a few of Satan's characteristics. Understand, Satan despises and hates all human beings. Satan's desire is to destroy every work of God, including His creation. Satan uses every kind of destructive activity possible to cause people to turn away from God and destroy themselves. He is referred to as the red dragon (bloodthirsty—**Revelation 12:3–10**), a roaring lion seeking someone to devour **(1 Peter 5:8)**, and the Apollyon, Abbadon (which means destroyer—**Revelation 9:11**).

Satan's main weapon is deception. Jesus calls him a murderer, the father of lies **(John 8:44)**, and an accuser (devil means *accuser*). One of the first examples of using lies and deception is with Eve in the garden by saying, **"You shall not surely die!" (Genesis 3:4).** The first lie was "you shall not die." Although it did not happen instantaneously, every human being throughout time has, in fact, died physically. There was another death being referred to that did happen instantaneously with the sin; it was "spiritual death."

The second deception was to get us to question the goodness of God.

> **For God knows that in the day that you eat from it your eyes will be opened, and you will be like God, knowing good and evil. (Genesis 3:5)**

To paraphrase this, Satan was basically saying, "God is trying to oppress you and keep you from reaching your full potential of being a god yourself!"

To understand the events written about in Exodus, as God used Moses to deliver the Israelites from Egyptian bondage, we must apply some principles that define the characteristics of the main players, namely, God, Moses, and the Pharaoh and now Satan. In chapter 1, I detailed evidence presented in the Scripture to know Moses's character, and in part the Pharaoh's. But what about God? His nature is spread throughout the universe, because it's all about Him! He's not contained in the essence of the Scripture alone, as the very creation itself glorifies Him. However, the Scripture is written in a way to give us intimate understanding, enabling us to relate to Him.

As you read of the plagues poured out on the nation of Egypt as recorded in Exodus, you will find God was, little by little, removing the Egyptians' comfort and provision to draw them into submission to the only true God. He was moving them toward a recognition that He alone was all-powerful and capable of supplying life, not the false gods they were currently worshipping. God wanted to give them life. He was gentle and patient with each plague, knowing all the while the outcome. He already knew they would refuse to acknowledge and worship Him.

During the first three plagues, God was merciful and only allowed the infliction to occur for a short period, even with the Pharaoh's hardened heart (**Exodus 7:14–8:19**). The next three plagues would only require the people to retreat to the land of Goshen in order to find reprieve. For God set apart His chosen in the land of Goshen from the Egyptian dwelling settlements (**Exodus 8:20–9:12**). The Pharaoh and the people were too proud to do so.

The seventh plague only required you to believe that God's word, given through Moses, was true and that the coming hail was going to happen. Therefore, placing all your valuables, servants, and livestock under shelter would have provided you safety. Some Egyptians did so and were spared along with the Israelites in the land of Goshen where no hail fell. Others chose not to believe and suffered great loss. Even so, God was still merciful as their late harvest crops were spared up to this point (**Exodus 9:13–9:26**).

The eighth plague of locusts (probably grasshoppers) would be sure to devour what remaining crops they had (**Exodus 10:1–20**).

They would have been spared had they just been willing to submit to the Lord's request in obedience. The plague of darkness (the ninth) was a direct message to the Egyptians that their most powerful and prominent god, the sun god Ra, would be no source of hope or safety. The Pharaoh would have found rest and even blessing if he would have chosen the repentance and obedience alternative.

However, this choice would have required the Pharaoh to relinquish his position as god of his own life and god over the lives of all under his authority. This Pharaoh would not do! In each of the plagues, God showed great mercy and patience with the Pharaoh who would be unwilling to trust in God. In spite of the Pharaoh's hardness of heart, even the Egyptians had an opportunity to avoid the full wrath of God through a choice to obey. Even so, God left the choosing open to each individual person. The plagues are designed to drive us back to God so that He can restore to us life.

Now comes the final plague. This one was designed to break the hardened will of the Pharaoh and the Egyptians as well. The death of the firstborn! God, as He did with all other plagues, provided a way of escape to those who would yield to Him in obedience. By belief in what was prophesied, the blood of the lamb over the doorposts would provide safety to all who dwell inside that household. This ordinance signified the coming Christ who would be the ultimate sacrificial Lamb for all men, for all time. Again, refusal to believe brought the death of the firstborn to everyone in the household, animals and all.

Now comes the question, did the LORD kill the firstborn? Now comes into play God the Father's character, which is what this book is about! As mentioned earlier in the chapter, God the Father's love was so great for the human race, He willingly sacrificed Himself to an excruciatingly horrible, painful, bloody death to save it. How does this kind of love line up with killing the firstborn? Seems harsh!

> **For I will go through the land of Egypt on that night, and will strike down all the firstborn in the land of Egypt, both man and beast; and against all the gods of Egypt I will execute judgments: I am the LORD. (Exodus 12:12 NASB)**

In this verse, it does appear that the Lord Himself would kill the firstborn. Moses wrote that God spoke this to him and referred to Himself in the first person: "I will go…and strike down all the firstborn…" Thinking deeply on other passages brushed throughout the Scripture paints a more understandable picture of His character in this event. Now compare this with **Exodus 12:23 (NASB)**.

> **For the LORD will pass through to smite the Egyptians; and when He sees the blood upon the lintel, and on the two doorposts, the LORD will pass over the door, and will not allow the destroyer to come in unto your houses to smite you.**

This verse begins to create a different picture. First of all, the Lord does pass through looking for the blood on the doorposts. This signifies that the Lord watches over us with hands-on care. He is also in complete control over all that takes place. Nothing will occur that He doesn't preside over. This verse also shows us that the LORD is not taking the life, but rather the "destroyer" taking the life. God has appointed angels to carry out His purposes. Who is the "destroyer"? Revelation 9 refers to him as the "king of the bottomless pit," "Abaddon, Apollyon." This is Satan, the death angel.

There are additional scriptures that present a common thread of theology regarding who takes away life. It's also seen throughout these additional passages.

> **By faith he kept the passover, and the sprinkling of the blood, that he who destroyed the firstborn might not touch them. (Hebrews 11:28 NASB)**

> **When the angel stretched out his hand toward Jerusalem to destroy it, the LORD relented from the calamity, and said to the angel that destroyed the people, "It is enough;**

now relax your hand. And the angel of the
LORD was by the threshing-floor of Araunah
the Jebusite."

Then David spoke to the LORD when he
saw the angel that was striking down the people, and said, "Behold, It is I who have sinned,
and it is I who have done wrong; but these
sheep, what have they done? Please let Thy
hand, be against me, and against my father's
house." (2 Samuel 24:16–17 NASB)

And the LORD sent an angel, who
destroyed every mighty warrior, commander
and officer in the camp of the king of Assyria.
So he returned in shame to his own land. And
when he had entered the temple of his god,
some of his own children killed him there with
the sword. (2 Chronicles 32:21 NASB)

And immediately an angel of the Lord
struck him, because he did not give God the
glory: and he was eaten by worms, and died.
(Acts 12:23 NASB)

Even in the light of all the scriptures just presented, some
will still try to hold to the belief God took the life of the firstborn.
Choosing also to believe God was angry. So my position would then
be, how would you explain these additional scriptures?

For we shall surely die, and are as water
spilled on the ground, which cannot be gathered up again; yet God does not take away life,
but plans ways so that the banished one may
not be cast out from Him. (2 Samuel 14:14
NASB; emphasis mine)

Also, in **Revelation 16:1, Judges 16:24, Psalm 17:4, and Jeremiah 4:7**. These passages clearly indicate that God may permit physical death to occur but does not execute it by His own hand. To understand His character of love better, consider other aspects of His nature. He is the protector. When death to an unbeliever does occur, God withdraws His divine protection, permitting the destroyer to take the life. God does not wish that any would perish but rather that all should come to repentance in order to have life (**2 Peter 3:9**). If the Lord permits death to occur to an unbeliever, it is because He knows this person would never accept God's offer of salvation. Therefore, it would be an act of mercy to not allow any more offspring be born and/or that should this person be allowed to live on, more evil and suffering of the innocent may occur. God is just. God is love (**1 John 4:8**). He is omniscient (all-knowing); therefore, all of His decisions are based out of love.

On the other side of this, He often permits a person to live long lives full of evil, causing great harm to the innocent, simply because He knows in the end, this person will come to repent and accept His salvation. King Manasseh was a good example of this (**2 Chronicles 33**). Or possibly that this unbeliever's child or grandchild will be saved; thus, it was necessary for evil men to prosper for a time so none of His chosen ones would be lost. To those who are believers in Christ, God allowing their death is not a punishment but a reward!

### Precious in the sight of the LORD are the death of His Saints. (Psalm 116:15)

And in **Luke 23:43,** Jesus, speaking to the dying thief on the cross next to Him, who professed Jesus as LORD, said, **"Today you shall be with me in paradise."**

For more concrete thought on this subject, consider another aspect of His nature. He is the Creator, Life-giver. To understand the attribute of God being a life-giver, examine some passages in both Old and New Testament. Christ, the Creator, breathed into the nostrils of the lifeless body, the "breath of life," and the lifeless body now became a living being.

**Then the LORD God formed man of dust from the ground, and breathed into his nostrils the breath of life; and man became a living being. (Genesis 2:7 NASB)**

Sin brought spiritual death (and ultimately physical death) to man at "the fall." Without getting too deep in the weeds on this subject, I believe the Scripture tells us very plainly that before Adam sinned in the garden, God's Spirit was present in man. As a result of what is referred to as "the fall," God's Spirit had to withdraw because God's nature is too pure to dwell with sin (**Habakkuk 1:13**). I've heard the words used describing Adam's and Eve's eyes being "opened"; knowing "they were naked" when they ate of the fruit in the garden was an event described as a sudden "stripping away." As a consequence of the sin of rebellion, God's Spirit was no longer able to indwell with the human spirit. The fall of mankind resulted in all kinds of unpleasant subsequent conditions of humanity (e.g., ruled by fear, darkened mind, weakened will, self-centered nature, enslaved to sin, spiritual and physical death, etc.).

**And when He had said this, He breathed on them and said "receive the Holy Spirit." (John 20: 22 NASB)**

A New Testament example of this same concept of "breathing the breath of life into man" is written in **John 20:20**, as Jesus addressed the apostles in the upper room. After Christ had paid the death penalty on behalf of those willing to put their trust in Him as their redeemer, and after Jesus's resurrection from the dead, Christ breathed again "life" (the Holy Spirit, or spiritual life) into those who believed (put their trust) in Him (**John 20:22**). Other scriptures such as **John 1:3, 10:10, 11:25, 14:6** and **1 John 5:12** all reveal there is no life outside of Christ. But this is talking about a spiritual life as well as an eternal physical life. In essence, sin brought spiritual death as God's Spirit withdrew from man. Christ's death penalty on behalf of the chosen believer restored God's Spirit into us again. We are now a living (spiritually) being, a "new creation."

Regarding creation, the Creator God sustains all that exist. **Colossians 1:16–17** says, "In Him all things hold together." **Hebrews 1:3** also communicates this idea, also speaking of Christ, He "upholds all things by the word of His power." This is to say that all the elemental substance of creation and life itself would not retain its existence without God holding it together. Without God's restraining protection from the forces of evil, all creation would be totally destroyed. All life would cease.

> **Then God said "Let us make man in Our image, according to Our likeness, and let them rule over the fish of the sea and over the birds of the sky and over the cattle and over all the earth, and over every creeping thing that creeps on the earth."**
>
> **God created man in His own image, In the image of God He created him, male and female He created them. (Genesis 1:26–27 NASB)**

Another important characteristic about God the Father's character is that He created us "in His image." What does this mean, created "in His image"? It's more complex than we may ever know on this side of eternity, but one aspect of it is that just as God is eternal in nature, so too is the spirit of man. Christians boast about having "eternal" life in our salvation by Christ, especially when trying to convince another person to become a Christian. However, I've had nonbelievers say something like "I think I'll just live life my own way. Even if there is a God, when I'm done living my own life and die, I'll just go in the grave, and that will be it. So what if I miss out on this so-called eternal life?" Then they would laugh and say, "It was good while it lasted!"

It doesn't really work that way. Even those who reject God's plan of salvation suffer darkness, torment, and separation from God—

eternally! This was made quite clear in Jesus's parable about life after death in **Matthew 25:31–46 and Luke 16:19–31**. This is eternal death. But the spirit of man is still yet an eternal being. We are either eternally with Him in abundant life or eternally separated from Him in eternal death. Even in death, He does not destroy the spirit of man. Jesus was even more direct when he spoke of this in **Mark 9:43–44** when talking about entering the unquenchable fire of hell "where their worm does not die." God is the life-giver, not the life taker!

To my knowledge, there is not one place in the Scripture that describes one of God's attributes as being a destroyer. There are several scriptures that speak of God destroying evil men, kings, nations, etc.; but even as I study many of those scriptures, I find there are several Hebrew words for "destroy." Most of those words can also actually mean to put out (away), cast off (out), remove, cut off, drive out, tear away, pluck up (out), pull up, set aside, etc. This would indicate the action of God setting aside for destruction or a removing of a ban on destruction. **Isaiah 34:2** (NASB) provides another example.

> **For the Lord's indignation is against all the nations, And *His* wrath against all their armies; He has utterly destroyed them, <u>He has given them over to slaughter</u>. (emphasis mine)**

The phrase "**He has given them over to slaughter**" indicates He doesn't destroy them with *His* own hand but rather gives them over to the destroying angel. The phrase "utterly destroyed" can also be interpreted as "put under the ban." This would be to "set aside or banned from His presence and protection." You may also want to notice in this passage that the word ***His*** in the phrase ***His* wrath** (referring to God) is in *italics*. This means it is not in the original text prior to translation but was later added for easier reading in English. The passage should simply say, "And wrath against all their armies…" It's not wise to add words to the Scripture! God's intent can be altered by doing so.

Many other verses indicate this same type of interpretation, such as **Jeremiah 25:9**, in which He again put them under the ban but allowed the actual destruction by Nebuchadnezzar, king of Babylon. Also, **Malachi 4:1** where He says, **"The day that is coming will set them ablaze."** Not that He would set them ablaze, but rather **"the day that is coming"** will set them ablaze. In the same chapter, verse 6 says, **"And He will restore the hearts of the fathers to their children, and the hearts of the children to their fathers, lest I come and smite the land with a curse."** The word "curse" again also means "to remove from the ban (on destruction)." Even the bowls of God's wrath in **Revelation 16** are carried out by angels. Could this be the angels who rebelled against God? Even though they are against God and know of their doom, they still must submit to His authority over them.

One verse that came to mind as I was researching this concept was **Matthew 10:28,** in which Jesus said, **"And do not fear those who kill the body, but are unable to kill the soul; but rather fear Him who is able to destroy both soul and body in hell."**

When I researched the word for "destroy" in Greek, **apollumi,** I found that it was made up of two root words, **apo**, which means to separate, set aside, and **olethros**, which means ruin, punishment. Together we get the meaning "to separate, set aside for destruction, ruin, punishment." Jesus was very careful to use words that described God's true nature and character. Meaning, He set aside and withdrew His protection, resulting in destruction.

It should also be said of the Scripture that the term "dispensation" reflects the idea that God has been revealing Himself to mankind in stages. As the earlier authors wrote about God, they wrote within their current knowledge and understanding of God. For example, in Job, there was a common misconception that a person's calamities were from God as a result of a person's own sin. God gave us in Job a corrected view of this false belief. Another example would be as John described in Revelation the coming doom of this earth. He described great locusts with a face of a man and tails that sting like a scorpion. We could possibly see these today to possibly be jet fighter planes or some future version of such. Also, what were described as arrows could be missiles, etc.

In the same way, God has been correcting false beliefs regarding His character and nature implied by earlier authors in the Scripture by later writings in both New and Old Testament books, especially in the gospels as Jesus (God in the flesh) spoke, correcting much more in wrong beliefs and understanding with His life and words. The authors of the New Testament wrote from what they learned and saw from following Jesus in person for at least three years.

How we view God the Father's character affects the way we view ourselves and treat others. If we believe God takes life, then we subconsciously believe that God is a killer or destroyer, and we can somehow justify that action. Some extremists believe murder is justified by this concept of God's character. I had a close friend, a fellow believer, once tell me during a discussion about the war on terrorism, "It's a good thing I'm not the president, because I would just keep shootin' till I'm out of bullets." It was meant to be a joke, and I laughed because it seemed funny (at the time), but there was an underlying belief about God's character in there somewhere. Why did God present the concept to us in the Scripture saying, "Vengeance is Mine says the LORD, I will repay"? It must be said that there is a difference between using a death penalty in enforcing a system of law and order to protect freedom in society. Otherwise, society would begin exercising a practice of being judge, jury, and executioner without due process.

In summary of this controversial subject, we should look at what Jesus has revealed about God's character, as He says, **"If you have seen me, you have seen the father."** I ask you to view those scriptures written about God destroying very closely in their entire context, then think of what Jesus has revealed to us about the nature of God as well as other misconceptions He corrected. Then, see if you can view Jesus's character as being a destroyer. God is love! Have you read **1 Corinthians 13** lately?

One more question yet to answer. Are the great storms, tornadoes, hurricanes, and earthquakes "acts of God"? God can certainly do as He wishes and has ultimate control over all of creation, which includes the weather patterns. But does He bring on these events in causing destruction and loss of life?

(Job 1:6–2:7)

These passages clearly present the evidence Satan has also been given power to affect the weather patterns and will use it to destroy mankind. My belief is that much of what we attribute to "acts of God" may be attributed to the "destroyer's" work. God may withdraw His divine protection and permit the destroyer to cause destruction and loss of life. Even in this, He protects His chosen ones. Even those who suffer loss of their physical life, the chosen ones are held safe in His presence, and those who never knew Him never would have repented had they been allowed to live on. Not one of His chosen will perish!

God can and has affected the weather patterns of this earth. I also believe there is a theological thread throughout the written Word supporting the theology that with the increase in sin, there is a direct increase in the decay of the earth, which would result in an increase in destructive weather patterns. To keep the focus on the main subject, I will avoid exploring that evidence here.

In the new heaven and new earth, there will be no more death, sickness, pain, or sorrow. These things weren't present in the present world until sin entered into the creation. These things are not God's desire, but He knows and uses their occurrences (they are a consequence of sin) as a time to teach us about the terrible results of sin and display to us His perfect character of love. Love so great He willingly gave Himself in death, in the form of Jesus Christ, to save His creation from death. God the Father's character is the life-giver, not that of the destroyer.

# THE GOLDEN CALF

As I WAS GROWING UP, one of my father's most frequently mentioned phrases was "You're going to reap what you sow, son!" I heard that phrase so often, it became ingrained in the control center of my brain that messages my bodily life functions, such as breathing, heartbeat, food digesting, etc. It's from **Galatians 6:7** (NASB), which says, **"Do not be deceived, God is not mocked; for whatever a man sows, this he will also reap."** This truth was probably more instrumental in saving my life, from death due to unbelief, than any other passage in the Bible. I felt that every time I experienced some kind of pain, weather physical or emotional, I just knew it had to be because of some previous sin that I had sowed. When the pain got severe enough, I would seek to God to find relief. It usually included making God promises I really didn't want to make or want to keep. I came to understand later in life my belief system was not totally accurate.

As I began an intensive study on the subject of "God the Father's character," I began to realize how this belief system influenced my view of God the Father. With this verse **(Galatians 6:7)** in mind, I had this picture of a huge powerful God who was sitting (or standing) there making retaliatory decisions for every sin I committed. I imagined I could hear Him saying things like "You shouldn't have done that! Now I'm going to have to make your life miserable to punish you." It's true we can't trick God, and we are going to reap a multifold harvest of all that we sow, but what is often misunderstood is the way God the Father views us and interacts with us in these areas of our lives. Without a proper perspective of "God the Father's" true character, we will mistreat others living a life of legalism and being judgmental. This causes great harm to ourselves and those around us, especially to those closest to us, our loved ones. It also damages our witness to the world and the cause of Christ.

There are many passages that seem to support the view of God being an angry, punishing God. One of the more prominent ones is in Exodus 32. Why? Is He really this way? How do we know?

> **Then Moses stood in the gate of the camp, and said, "Whoever is for the Lord, *come* to me!" And all the sons of Levi gathered together to him.**
>
> **He said to them, "Thus says the Lord, the God of Israel, 'Every man *of you* put his sword upon his thigh, and go back and forth from gate to gate in the camp, and kill every man his brother, and every man his friend, and every man his neighbor.'"**
>
> **So the sons of Levi did as Moses instructed, and about three thousand men of the people fell that day. (Exodus 32:26–28 NASB)**

As I read this passage in **Exodus 32** during the earlier years of my life, I had no problem with it. I viewed God as a Judge who was righteous, and destroying evil was His business. As my relationship with Christ drew more intimate, I became conflicted and began to question passages as this one. In chapter 3 of this book, I outlined the idea that the God of the Israelites and Jesus Christ, the "I Am," were one and the same. I thought of the character of Jesus, and His love toward others, such as the sick, the helpless, the blind, and the oppressed. Then I thought of the woman at the well, who was an adulteress. Also, the woman the Pharisees brought to Jesus who was "caught in the very act." Both of these women were sentenced in the Mosaic law to death. But Jesus's response to them was entirely different than the passage we just read seemed to indicate.

I've heard this apparent contradiction justified by theologians as different dispensations, which is the belief that God has dealt with man in different ways in different periods. I do believe this as well for the most part, but when we begin to investigate the character of God, we must remember the Scripture has made it clear that He is the same yesterday, today, and forever (**Hebrews 1:12, 13:8; Malachi 3:6; James 1:17**). Jesus, who is God in the flesh, said, "He who has seen Me has seen the Father" (**John 14:9**) and "I and the Father are One" (**John 10:30** NASB).

In light of this, it becomes increasingly difficult to ignore these truths and believe God commanded Moses to slay each one his brother and neighbor. But the Scripture seems to indicate this in Exodus 32, or does it? Studied closely in its entire context, it becomes apparent there is a distinct difference between who Moses thought God was and who God revealed Himself to be. Before you hang me or burn me at the stake for heresy, please allow me to present the evidence given in the Scripture.

Let me set the stage for you. The Israelites have been moving through the desert for nearly three months at this point. They were miraculously saved from certain slaughter by the Egyptians. Being trapped between the Red Sea and the surrounding mountains, God parted the Red Sea, providing a passage of escape while destroying the ensuing Egyptians. They were faint from lack of water, food, and shelter. God miraculously provided them water and manna from heaven every day for weeks. God gave them victory in battle against the Amalekites. It's been a rough three months! But the Almighty God has been faithful to supply all their needs.

> **And Moses went up unto God, and the LORD called to him from the mountain, saying, "Thus you shall say to the house of Jacob, and tell the sons of Israel:**
>
> **You yourselves have seen what I did to the Egyptians, and how I bore you on eagles' wings, and brought you to Myself.**
>
> **<u>Now then, if ye will indeed obey My voice, and keep My covenant, then ye shall be Mine own possession from among all peoples</u>: for all the earth is Mine;**

**and you shall be to Me a kingdom of priests, and a holy nation. These are the words which thou shalt speak unto the children of Israel."**

**So Moses came and called for the elders of the people, and set before them all these words which the LORD had commanded him.**

**<u>And all the people answered together, and said, "All that the LORD has spoken we will do</u>" And Moses brought back the words of the people to the LORD. (Exodus 19:3–8 NASB; emphasis mine)**

Moses ascends up and down the mountain several times meeting with the LORD. He becomes the intercessor relaying messages between God and the people. God commands Moses to remind the people about God's goodness, His miracles to save them, His heart of compassion, His desire to love them as His own, and His purpose for their lives as witnesses to the world of His existence and character. Then God commands Moses to "consecrate" himself to prepare to meet with Him on the third day. It's in this meeting, in God's presence, the Ten Commandments were written. God could choose anyone on earth. He specifically chose them, the most downtrodden and helpless of the world. Sounds like the chosen body of Christ today!

God sends through Moses a love letter to the Israelites, verifying His actions and intent for His relationship with them. Sounds much like an offer for marriage. However, in **verse 5**, there's one small catch. He specifically asks them to not cheat on Him by asking them, "If you will indeed obey My voice and keep My covenant, then you shall be My own possession…" It must also be said here that the phrase "My own possession" can also be interpreted to mean "My special treasure." The people responded with a blind "All that the LORD has spoken we will do," even though they haven't yet seen what is being asked of them regarding the "laws" to be obeyed and "covenant" to be kept. They haven't seen the Ten Commandments yet.

During this first visit, the LORD tells Moses to tell the people to "consecrate" themselves, in preparation for God's descending to the mountaintop. The word "consecrate" means "to set aside, to be holy, to cleanse, and to make pure." God also gives specific instruction to the people to not ascend the mountain! Not to even touch the base of it. If they did, the results wouldn't be good.

**He said to the people, "Be ready for the third day; do not go near a woman." (Exodus 19:15 NASB)**

I didn't write it. This means to not approach in close-enough proximity to touch. To understand this request requires an ability to understand by experience what happens to a man's character, focus, and heart when his thoughts are on a male-female physical relationship. His mind becomes consumed by the thought of the pleasure. He loses the ability to keep his focus on anything else effectively. His willpower to exhibit godly character and physical strength is severely weakened. It could be just me, but I'm believing it's a common problem with all men. "That's my story, and I'm sticking to it!"

If a man's physical advances are resisted or spurned, his self-confidence is shaken, often to the point of total collapse both mentally and physically. We cannot give our total attention and affection to God while our attention is focused toward the male-female relationship. Yet our culture today is permeated with this mindset of sex. We are bombarded with it in movies, TV shows, advertising, talk shows, etc. Satan knows this weakness in us and is waging an effective war on God's chosen. It is a beautiful thing within the bounds of marriage. However, even within that context, intentional effort needs to be taken to not allow that pleasure in the relationship to replace dependence on the relationship with God.

**Now Mount Sinai *was* all in smoke because the Lord descended upon it in fire; and its smoke ascended like the smoke of a**

furnace, and the whole mountain quaked violently.

When the sound of the trumpet grew louder and louder, Moses spoke and God answered him with thunder.

The LORD came down on Mount Sinai, to the top of the mountain; and the LORD called Moses to the top of the mountain, and Moses went up.

Then the LORD spoke to Moses, "Go down, warn the people, so that they do not break through to the LORD to gaze, and many of them perish.

Also let the priests who come near to the LORD consecrate themselves, or else the LORD will break out against them."

Moses said to the LORD, "The people cannot come up to mount Sinai, for You warned us, saying, 'Set bounds about the mountain and consecrate it.'"

Then the Lord said to him, "Go down and come up *again*, you and Aaron with you; but do not let the priests and the people break through to come up to the LORD, or He will break forth upon them."

So Moses went down to the people and told them. (Exodus 19:18–25 NASB)

Once these instructions were carried out by Moses and the people, Moses brings the people out of the camp to meet God at the foot of the mountain. This is interesting. Looking at what Moses said to the LORD in **verse 23**, I can just imagine what was going through Moses's mind here. Probably something like "I just climbed all the way up here and you want me to go all the way back down again and tell them to consecrate themselves again and not come near the mountain again! Do you realize I'm eighty years old? Let's just get on with this! You probably forgot, Lord, I already told them all that." Nevertheless, the Lord told Moses to go down and come up again.

Moses obeys. While Moses was at the base of the mountain, God spoke to him in the presence of the people. The people were only able to hear the sound of loud thunder. During this communication, the Ten Commandments were first given by God to Moses after he and Aaron had climbed the mount **(verse 24)**. In addition to the Ten Commandments, ordinances for the people regarding cultural human relationships, personal injuries, property rights, sundry laws, laws of the Sabbath, the feasts, and instructions for conquering foreign lands were also given.

In **Exodus 20:20–22,** Moses indicated that God was testing them. God is a Holy God! God instructed Moses to warn the people to consecrate themselves. Twice! It's no small thing to be in the presence of the "Most High God," Creator of the universe! The manner God used to reveal His presence was in the form of a dark cloud large enough to cover an entire mountaintop. Speaking to Moses in loud thunder was to awaken the people's attention of God's power. Recognizing His awesome greatness is essential in instilling in us a desire to be obedient. He wanted the Israelites to know that He is the Only God of all heaven, and He wanted their obedience! Speaking to Moses in this manner validated before the people Moses had God's given authority.

After the loud thunder ceased, **Exodus 24:3** tells us that Moses "recounted to the people all the words of the Lord." The people responded with one voice, "All the words which the Lord has spoken we will do!" And just in case their hearing was impaired, due to all the loud thunder, Moses also wrote the words down. Then they offered burnt offerings to the Lord as peace offerings.

> **He sent young men of the sons of Israel, and they offered burnt offerings and sacrificed young bulls as peace offerings to the Lord.**
> **Moses took half of the blood and put *it* in basins, and the *other* half of the blood he sprinkled on the altar.**

> Then he took the book of the covenant
> and read *it* in the hearing of the people; and
> they said, "All that the LORD has spoken we
> will do, and we will be obedient!" (Exodus
> 24:5–7 NASB)

**Exodus 24:5–7** provides additional detail. <u>**Four times**</u> God commanded the people to not worship any other god, make images of the false gods, or serve them! <u>**Three times**</u> the people have now responded with "All that the LORD has spoken we will do!" They even were told twice that violators would be put to death and utterly destroyed!

Moses has been in the presence of God on three different occasions by going up Mount Sinai. Each trek up the mountain, God presented more information to establish a form of worship and relationship between His chosen people and the Almighty God. On the third trip, Moses stayed in the presence of God on the mountain for forty days. God has just given him the stone tablets of the Ten Commandments. Meanwhile, back at the ranch (camp), the people are becoming restless. They complained to Aaron that this Moses has disappeared, so now there is a need to "make gods who will go before us."

> And when the people saw that Moses
> delayed to come down from the mountain, the
> people assembled about Aaron, and said to
> him, "Come, make us gods, who will go before
> us; as for this Moses, the man who brought us
> up from the land of Egypt, we do not know
> what is become of him." (Exodus 32:1 NASB)

Notice the plural word "gods." Their natural instinct was to return to the form of religion they knew before, which was the Egyptian worship of many gods! One for each need or desire. They were not yet willing (or able) to attribute the previous miracles they witnessed to YHWH. When they believed Moses was not coming back, they immediately began searching for other "gods." This fact is evidence they were worshipping Moses, not YHWH!

We are the same today as well. Some people who lack an intimate relationship with the indwelling Spirit of God worship pastors, Bible teachers, popes, money, possessions, power, and other forms of religious idols. When the pastor sins (and they all do), they start their search for another god. Like the Israelites, it is sometimes in the form of a man or maybe of materialistic idols. Now examine the one that the Israelites chose as represented by the "golden calf."

This was a worship of the Egyptian god Apis, the sacred bull god of Memphis. It was believed to be the reincarnated god of Ptah, the creator god. Archeologists have discovered several burial tombs with mummified bull calf's in and around Memphis. This god is associated with many other Egyptian false gods including Osiris, Isis, Hathor, Horus, Amon, Min, and Re.

Throughout history, different civilizations have served a form of this same god prior to this Egyptian period. The Canaanites called him by several names including Molech, Chemosh, Chiun, Shamesh, Ashtarte, and Baal. These gods were variations from the most ancient form of the moon god named Sin. The Canaanites were under Assyro-Babylonian dominance from 3000 BCE to 1700 BCE, and their influence was so great that all correspondence with Egypt and the Pharaoh was conducted in the Babylonian language. The Egyptian period in which the Israelite exodus took place is believed to be approximately 1447 BCE. Thus, the earlier civilizations would have influenced later civilizations in their forms of idol worship, especially since they were interacting in trade and commerce. The name of the moon god Sin formed the basis for the Canaanite names Sinai and the Wilderness of Sin.

This god was the god of sex and the god of fertility. The form of worship consisted of sexually immoral activities, such as orgies, male and female temple prostitution, and human sacrifice. It was believed in that culture that the moon god Sin caused "catatonia" or madness in children. Hence, lunacy is associated with this deity. It could be very likely that the lunacy was a result of incest. This was basically a god of pleasure and prosperity. Just watch the TV and movies, and you can easily see the worship of the "golden calf" in our own culture today.

A ritual of the worship of Baal was to sacrifice alive newborn infants on an altar, heated to red hot! The newborn infants were born from temple prostitutes nearest to the time of worship. This was in hopes of receiving from this "god" the blessing of abundant crops (source of income) and a prosperous future. We call it "abortion" or "pro-choice" today. Essentially the same thing, a sacrifice of the infant for unhindered education, career, pursuit of wealth, and self-serving happiness. More free sex without responsibility.

> **Then the LORD spoke to Moses, "Go down at once, for your people, whom you brought up from the land of Egypt, have corrupted *themselves*.**
> **They have quickly turned aside from the way which I commanded them. They have made for themselves a molten calf, and have worshiped it and have sacrificed to it and said, 'This is your god, O Israel, who brought you up from the land of Egypt!'" (Exodus 32:7–8 NASB)**

What I want you to notice is the phrase **"and have sacrificed to it,"** in reference to the golden calf. They left Egypt with **"a mixed multitude…,"** **"a very large number of livestock" (Exodus 12:38)**. This tells us that not all who left Egypt were Israelites. They could have been Egyptians who found favor with the Israelites (**Leviticus 24:10–16**) or fellow slaves captured from military conquests of other surrounding Canaanite tribes. This was the practice during this period. In any case, certain livestock was considered sacred, and sacrificing them would be **"what is considered an abomination to the Egyptians" (Exodus 8:26 NASB)**.

This is why the people were complaining about having no meat and only manna, while they were surrounded by livestock! If the mixed multitude were from surrounding Canaanite tribes, they would've also considered livestock as sacred (reincarnated relatives). Here's my point, if sacrificing animals to the golden calf was considered an abomination to the culture, what were they sacrificing? Humans? Especially since this was the worship practice of the culture of these particular gods!

This was made clear in **Leviticus 18:21, 26–30, 20:1–5**, and **Deuteronomy 12:31**. These ordinances given in Leviticus immediately followed the golden calf incident during Moses's second forty-day ascension up Mount Sinai. God was laying out the laws and ordinances that were to govern His chosen nation. They were being reprogrammed from the corrupt cultures they had been exposed to for 430 years. The Scripture doesn't completely make this clear, but strong evidence points to this possibility.

The LORD in **Exodus 32:9** calls the Israelites a stiff-necked people. In Hebrew, this also means a "cruel, hardened, sorrowful, and stubborn" people. It also means they were unwilling to lift their head up to acknowledge God as God, nor were they willing to bow their head down low in humble repentance and submission to Him.

Now it's easier to understand why the LORD was displeased. Not only was He **not** recognized as their God within their hearts, but He had just sent them this love letter, and they rejected Him. Also, you might need to be reminded that God had twice already miraculously supplied water when they were in need and had been providing manna daily for nearly three months right up to the morning they forsook Him for the "golden calf." They returned to the corrupt and degrading worship of these false gods. They were sacrificing humans to Satan essentially.

Moses was caught in the middle, as a mediator between God and the Israelites. He feels the LORD's pain of being rejected by the people, as well as pity for the Israelites, knowing their feebleness and their lack of understanding. Moses found understanding God very difficult himself.

The next set of events is much too important to pass over. On his third ascension up the mountain, God gave Moses specific instructions. The first two times, no one was allowed to even touch the base of the mountain. This time God gave instructions for Aaron, Nadab, Abihu, and seventy of the elders of Israel to go partway up the mountain with him. Then Moses was to ascend the rest of the way alone. Aside from the fact Moses may have been concerned with being eighty years old and dreading a third climb without someone to carry him back down, God had specific plans for Moses to establish a royal priesthood to minister to the people.

The blood sacrifice has now atoned for their sin and allowed them to approach the throne of God. But only the high priest, Moses, could approach the very presence of God. This was a foreshadowing of what is in place today. That is, Christ is our High Priest, and we are His royal priesthood (**1 Peter 2:9**) covered by His blood sacrifice of Himself for our sins. Because of our penalty of sin being paid in full by Christ's death, we can now approach the throne of God and speak to Him directly.

Comparing **Exodus 24:9–10** to **Exodus 33:19–20**, **John 1:18**, **5:37**, **Colossians 1:15**, and **1 Timothy 6:16**, it's clear that God is invisible, and no man has ever seen God (NASB). No man can see God and live. Who, then, is appearing to Moses, Aaron, Nadab, Abihu, and the seventy elders of Israel? This would be Jesus Christ! We already know that He is the "I Aᴍ" that appeared to Moses in the burning bush. Ezekiel describes Him in a similar manner in **Ezekiel 1:26** and **10:1–2.** He also appeared to Abraham and Daniel as King Melchizedek.

While Moses was on the mountain this third time, God gave instructions regarding the tabernacle and all the elements of corporate worship for the people. It was at this time that the tablets of the Ten Commandments were inscribed in stone by the finger of God. God tells Moses to "go down at once, for your people whom you brought up from the land of Egypt, have corrupted themselves."

> **Now then let me alone, that my anger**
> **may burn against them, and that I may destroy**
> **them: and I will make of you a great nation.**
> **(Exodus 32:10 NASB)**

Is God teaching Moses that it is acceptable to kill when you get angry? No, I believe God is attempting to show Moses that there are two ways to deal with people who do not know God. One of which

God clearly mentions here, to wipe them out and start over. The other method we must search a bit deeper for. Notice that He tells Moses in **verse 7** that they are "your people that you brought up out of Egypt." Moses's response in **verse 11** is quite interesting.

> **And Moses entreated the LORD his God, and said, O LORD, why does Thine anger burn against Thy people, whom Thou has brought out of the land of Egypt with great power and with a mighty hand? (Exodus 32:11 NASB; emphasis mine)**

Here, Moses says (paraphrased), "Wait a minute! These are not my people—they are your people." And in **verse 12**, he says that "if you destroy these people, then the Egyptians will view you as an evil God who destroyed his own people." Then He reminds God that He has already promised that He would multiply Abraham's descendants and bring them into the inheritance. In other words, he is reminding God not to go back on His word. Then Moses asks God to change His mind and spare the people.

> **For I, the LORD, do not change; there-fore you, O sons of Jacob, are not consumed. (Malachi 3:6 NASB)**

The verse in Malachi makes clear that God doesn't change His mind. He is omniscient (all-knowing); therefore, all His thoughts and actions are perfect. He makes no error in judgment. I believe God is revealing to Moses the second option as opposed to destroy-ing them and starting over. That is to take responsibility for them, to intercede for them. Take them under your wing to teach and nurture them in the ways of God so that they may live.

In a way, He's using a type of child psychology to show Moses that killing and starting over may not be the best choice of action, as Moses took when He killed the Egyptian for being unrighteous. He is telling Moses that if he doesn't intercede "now" for them on their behalf, then He will have no other choice but to allow their destruction. Moses is willing to intercede on behalf of the people at this point, but remember, he hasn't come down from the mountain and seen the sin of the people yet!

> **And it came about, as soon as he came near the camp, that he saw the calf and the dancing: and Moses' anger burned, and he threw the tablets from his hands, and shattered them at the foot of the mountain. (Exodus 32:19 NASB)**

> **And Aaron said, Do not let not the anger of my lord burn: you know the people yourself, that they are prone to evil. (Exodus 32:22 NASB)**

> **Then Moses stood in the gate of the camp, and said, "Whoever is for the LORD, come to me!" And all the sons of Levi gathered together to him.**
> **And he said unto them, "Thus saith the LORD, the God of Israel, 'Every man of you put his sword upon his thigh, and go back and forth from gate to gate in the camp, and kill every man his brother, and every man his friend, and every man his neighbor.'"**
> **So the sons of Levi did as Moses instructed: and about three thousand men of the people fell that day. (Exodus 32:26–28 NASB)**

Now we see the real Moses. No question about it, Moses was mad that day. Moses takes charge and really intercedes on behalf of God here (or at least so he thinks). He's supposed to be interceding on behalf of the people! Maybe, not so much this day, everyone can have a bad day. So much for the pious, compassionate attitude he had toward the people before he came down from the mountain. The question is, did God really tell Moses to kill every man his brother and every man his neighbor?

Look closely at these passages again and examine them in their entire context. First, notice that **verse 19** tells us that "Moses' anger burned." We already knew that He had a problem with anger as we studied in chapter 1 about Moses's character. Moses's brother, Aaron, also reinforced the idea that he had witnessed this "out-of-control anger" in Moses before **(verse 22)**. If Moses was carrying out the LORD God's perfect justice, why didn't he slay Aaron? Aaron made the golden calf! The passage in **James 1:20** (NASB) makes it clear that man's anger does not accomplish God's will.

> For the anger of man does not achieve the righteousness of God.

I've read this passage many times, but I noticed something in **verse 28** I had not seen before. It says, "The sons of Levi did according to <u>Moses</u> word," <u>not according to the word of the LORD</u>! Interesting. Moses wrote this book. What's up here? There's more evidence as well.

> **And it came about on <u>the next day</u>, that Moses said unto the people, "You yourselves have committed a great sin: and now I am going up to the LORD; perhaps I can make atonement for your sin.**
>
> **Then Moses returned to the LORD, and said, "Alas, <u>this</u> people has committed a great sin, and have made a god of gold for themselves.**
>
> **But now, if thou wilt, forgive their sin— and if not, blot me out from Thy book which Thou hast written! (Exodus 32:30–32 NASB; emphasis mine)**

Apparently, Moses had not sought the LORD in prayer yet. He doesn't do this until verses 30–31—THE NEXT DAY! Moses finally realizes that fixing this tragedy rests in the LORD. After all, the bloodshed has settled his emotions. He is now willing to intercede on behalf of the people. Moses's only problem, at this point, is that He doesn't know the character of God the Father well enough to teach and nurture the Israelites in the LORD's ways. When Moses makes his plea to the LORD on the people's behalf, his position that the people were God's people has changed. Now they are referred to as "this people." In Moses's thinking, they are no longer God's, nor his people, but rather "those" people. In other words, He was saying to God, "It's just you and me, God, that are righteous. 'Those' people, however, need forgiveness." He doesn't see his own corrupted view of righteousness yet. God's response to Moses's intercession on behalf of the people is astounding.

> **And the LORD said to Moses, "Whoever has sinned against me, I will blot him out of My book.**
> **But go now, lead the people where I told you. Behold, My angel shall go before you; nevertheless, in the day when I punish, I will punish them for their sin."**
> **Then the LORD smote the people, because of what they did with the calf, which Aaron had made. (Exodus 32:33–35 NASB; emphasis mine)**

He corrected Moses on several issues. First, He informed Moses that each person will bear the responsibility for their own sin. The person whose sin debt remains unpaid would be blotted out from God's book of life. Moses's willingness to be sacrificed on behalf of their sin was not acceptable. Moses was not sinless, or unblemished. Only God Himself, in the form of Jesus Christ, could provide the perfect sinless blood sacrifice for sin on our behalf.

Second, He tells Moses, "By the way, Moses, when I punish the people for their sin, I will punish them, **not you!**" Then the LORD smote the people **(verse 35)**. If God were commanding Moses to kill the Israelites in **verse 27**, He would be issuing a double punishment again **(verse 35)**. If this were true, it would be like God, in effect, was saying, "Now that you remind me of how bad 'those' people were, I didn't kill enough of them. I'm gonna slay some more of them!" This would imply that God has out-of-control emotions and desired to punish twice for the same sin. It would also indicate that God made a mistake in not issuing a proper degree of punishment to bring discipline the first time. This is not possible, as God is perfect and never makes a mistake.

It must be emphasized here that God knows all things. He is omniscient. God can decide to withdraw His life-sustaining protection from man, thus allowing harm or physical death to occur. Those who were slain by Moses didn't change the LORD's plan to establish a holy nation. God was using the event to purify the Levitical priesthood from those who wouldn't serve Him alone. I believe Moses carrying out what he thought was God's will (killing three thousand people) on his own was not in the LORD's plan. Just a couple of direct passages give us this understanding.

> **Never take your own revenge, beloved, but leave room for the wrath *of God*, for it is written, "VENGEANCE IS MINE, I WILL REPAY," says the Lord. (Romans 12:19 NASB)**

> **Let the wicked forsake his way, and the unrighteous man his thoughts; and let him return to the LORD, and he will have compassion upon him; and to our God, for he will abundantly pardon.**
> **For my thoughts are not your thoughts, neither are your ways My ways, saith the LORD.**
> **For as the heavens are higher than the earth, so are my ways higher than your ways,**

**and My thoughts than your thoughts. (Isaiah 55:7–9 NASB)**

Man does not know enough of God's will and nature to act on God's behalf. People often think they can carry out His will righteously. It's a serious mistake to think this way. Instead, we should be willing to seek the LORD on all issues and decisions we face and leave the action to God. And when it comes to discipline of another person (outside of the God-given parenting responsibility and the institution of the rule of law ordained by governments), it is God alone who is to make judgments on what discipline, if any, is to be given. Governments are to carry out judicial enforcement of law based on a standard as provided for by God.

What about **Exodus 32:27**, when Moses speaks to the people, "Thus says the Lord…go and kill every man his brother, friend, and neighbor." How can the words of the Bible be considered as truth and have this phrase when it may not have been the LORD's command to kill the people? The LORD said of the commandment to "not have any other gods before Me, you shall not worship them, make any graven image of them, nor serve them" (paraphrased), that violators should be put to death! Moses's heart was of a righteous fervor for the LORD God. He had the God-given authority of government, and the rule of law established by God. However, it was not God's will for it to be carried out in an "out of control" emotion of anger! Moses did not seek the LORD's will in the matter before acting.

Immediately following this communication with the LORD, Moses again ascends the mountain and fasts another forty days. He learns a bit more of God's true character. In this process, Moses realizes, at least in part, that God is attempting to teach him something new about His character: how to love people who are in an evil condition, having lost their way. You can see this in the intimate conversation between Moses and God in chapters 33 and 34.

**Then Moses said to the LORD, "See, You say to me, 'Bring up this people!' But You Yourself have not let me know whom You will**

**send with me. Moreover, You have said, 'I have known you by name, and you have also found favor in My sight.'**

**Now therefore, I pray You, if I have found favor in Your sight, let me know Your ways that I may know You, so that I may find favor in Your sight. Consider too, that this nation is Your people."**

**"For how then can it be known that I have found favor in Your sight, I and Your people? Is it not by Your going with us, so that we, I and Your people, may be distinguished from all the *other* people who are upon the face of the earth?" (Exodus 33:12–13, 16 NASB)**

Here, Moses acknowledges several things. He's realizing God is wanting him to nurture these people, but he knows that he doesn't have the understanding and ability to carry it out. Then Moses, realizing something isn't right with his own view of the situation, asks the LORD to "let me know your ways, that I may know you." He asks the LORD to teach him His ways so that he will know the true character of God the Father, rather than his corrupted view of fatherhood.

You might also notice Moses's own view of himself as righteous began to change. Previously he viewed himself as righteous with God in referring to "this" people. In asking God to take the responsibility of fathering the people ("Thy people"), Moses finally begins to align himself <u>with</u> the same level of righteousness or lack of righteousness as the people ("I and Thy people"). God reveals His intimate presence by allowing the train of His Shekinah glory to pass in front of Moses.

**And the LORD, the LORD God, compassionate and gracious, slow to anger, and abounding in lovingkindness and truth, who keeps lovingkindness for thousands, who forgives iniquity, transgression and sin; yet He will by no means leave the guilty unpunished,**

> **visiting the iniquity of the fathers upon the children, and upon the grandchildren to the third and fourth generations. (Exodus 34:6–7 NASB)**

The first thing God teaches Moses about His true character of "God the Father" is that of love, a heart of compassion, and forgiveness. This is in contrast to Moses's idea of God's character of being a harsh God of recompense. Now we see God the Father's character is the same as that of Jesus Christ. This is why Jesus forgave the adulterous women rather than stone them, as the law required. Moses's response to this revelation was intense.

> **And Moses made haste, to bow low toward the earth and worship.**
> **And he said, If now I have found favor in Thy sight, O Lord, I pray, let the Lord go alongside in <u>our</u> midst; even though the people are so obstinate; and do Thou pardon <u>our</u> iniquity and <u>our</u> sin, and take <u>us</u> as Thine own possession. (Exodus 34:8–9 NASB).**

Moses then bows his head low in repentant worship **(verse 9)**. He asks the LORD to go alongside in **"<u>our</u>"** midst, to pardon **"<u>our</u>"** sin (his and the people's). Then he asks God to take **"<u>us</u>"** (him and the people) as His own possession. Moses now realizes his proper place. Instead of seeing himself as righteous with God and the people in need of God's forgiveness, for the first time he sees himself as unrighteous as the people. They were all destined for punishment (death) and in need of forgiveness and salvation.

In closing, please allow me to summarize. God already knew of Moses's corrupt childhood abuse that caused him to have such a harsh view of God the Father. God was extremely gentle with Moses in teaching him the truth about His loving nature. We do reap what we sow, but God grieves in pain with us when we sow evil, knowing that the pain of reaping will hurt His precious creation. He understands why we sin, just as he understood why Moses killed three thousand men out of anger. The Pharaoh could have been driven by the same type of out-of-control emotions, acting harshly toward his subjects.

I believe Moses made a mistake in acting on his own emotion before seeking God's presence. I believe we act out in this way also, and it is a lifelong process of taking on the character of God the Father. God is a God of love and compassion, slow to anger, and forgiving. Just as important as these characteristics is the fact that He is all-knowing, omniscient. He could see Moses's heart. As corrupted as his emotional state might have been, God could see the righteous heart of Moses.

God yearns to gently teach us the truth that we may be able to turn and walk a path of life, eternal joy, and rest, rather than a path of destruction and reaping destruction. God takes no pleasure in seeing the reaping of what we are sowing **(Lamentations 3:33)**. He also knows it's a necessary part of His plan to save some from (eternal) death. His preference is to teach us His true character of love that we might display it toward others. We are to be so Christlike and holy that others may also be drawn to Him and His kind of love. This is what He was trying to teach Moses about interceding for the people, nurturing the people, and teaching them in the understanding of the LORD's ways.

Those who would kill abortion doctors, hate homosexuals, murder by terrorism, and shun people who may have committed open sin need to remind themselves of the true character of God the Father. Husbands and fathers who abuse their wife and children in the name of some corrupted idea of righteousness need again to seek the true character of God the Father, who is the same yesterday, today, and forever.

# THE "SHEKINAH" GLORY

HAVE YOU EVER REALLY CONSIDERED what the term "omniscient" means? Most of us know it means "all-knowing," but I mean have we really attempted to grasp what all-knowing is? Our small limited minds cannot even begin to truly understand its depth. To get a slight glimpse into understanding omniscience, let's take just a minute and ponder some simple data. Think of the complexity of living organisms. A single human sperm cell has roughly a trillion atoms (1,000,000,000,000). That's one million times one million. Or a single brain (neuronal) cell contains roughly 175 trillion neurons.[3] Think of how many different functions take place in a single cell. The responses (chemical, neurological, etc.) that occur in the simplest cell are believed to exceed over one hundred thousand per second.

Now consider how different stimuli might affect a living cell differently. For example, the *Mycoplasma pneumonia* is a small single-cell bacterium that causes atypical pneumonia in humans. This bacterium is incredibly flexible and has the ability to adjust its metabolism to drastic changes in environmental conditions. It adapts very quickly to survive! How can all probable environmental conditions have been known and anticipated well enough to preprogram into a cell its capability to react to these many different environmental variations well enough to survive unchanged throughout all time? The author of the article that identified this fact wrote, "Those are the things that not even the simplest organism can do without and that have remained untouched by millions of years of evolution—the bare essentials of life."[4]

By the way, I am by no means a scientist or an expert on any of the subjects outlined in this chapter opening. In addition, I'm not a fan of the millions of years of evolutionary science. This theory simply suggests that our complex earth, universe, and all its millions of living creatures just eventually happened to come together in the exact right combination of elements, substance, temperature, light, gravity, density, timing, and all other variable conditions to form life. Then they evolve (in a devolving creation) over millions, if not billions, of years into our current existence as we know it.

I lack faith in this theory mainly because the mathematical science doesn't support its probability. Here's a simple example of this. Take apart a working mousetrap. Put all the seven individual separate pieces into a paper bag and shake it. Then look in there and see if it fell together to be able to work. How many times would you have to shake it before all the pieces happen to fall together in exactly the correct secured alignment to become a fully functional working mousetrap? Or for a bigger experiment, try a computer. The creation is too complex. The mathematical probability verifies it's a mathematical impossibility. In addition, there's no explanation for where all the elements (goo) came from either. Besides, God's written Word doesn't support it. I have more faith in God than man's limited understanding!

That's just a snippet of one subject—biology. Now add all the thoughts and emotions that occur in one human heart and mind in an hour. Now multiply that times approximately 7.7 billion people.[5] God isn't stressed yet. Now add the vast universe of billions of stars and galaxies. Louie Giglio's video "Indescribable" does a good job of expressing this awareness. Then there's the rest of what we don't know of the entire universe. God is fully aware of even the slightest movement in the smallest microscopic creature in existence too small for the human eye to detect. God is still not overworked or close to reaching a physical limit. I think you get the idea. The reason I felt inclined to pursue this line of thought was to begin getting you acquainted with just one of God the Father's characteristics: **omniscience**.

**Are not two sparrows sold for a cent? And yet not one of them will fall to the ground apart from your Father.**

**But the very hairs of your head are all numbered.**
**So do not fear; you are more valuable than many sparrows. (Matthew 10:29–31 NASB)**

In light of the awesomeness of this inconceivable characteristic, I find it amusing to realize what truly fascinates humans today, such as a magician or a juggler who can manage a few items all at once. When I was a young boy, I was watching a musical special on TV when one of my favorite guitarists, Jim Stafford (pre-Jimmy Page–Led Zeppelin), played two different songs simultaneously on the guitar. I watched in utter fascination as he played the melodies with great precision at the same time. I kept listening for a mistake or a missed note. It never came. This has been one of the strongest memories of my teenage years. He did two things at once, but when we compare this event with the awesomeness of God's omniscience, we really should laugh at how limited we are in our thinking. Or laugh at our smallness of mind. How can we even begin to think thoughts like "God doesn't care or even consider someone like me important"? Or He's too busy, or not big enough.

In this chapter, I want to focus the attention on one example of many of this characteristic, "omniscience," God provided in His written Word. In Hebrew, this is referred to as the "pishot" and the "remez." The "pishot" is the surface meaning, while the "remez" is the hidden meaning. He does this by the use of dual meanings in words. This in fact is used throughout the Scripture.

One reason He used this in the Scripture was to validate that the Bible is truly divinely inspired by God alone. Forty different men were used to write the Bible. With man's limited ability, he would be unable to carry out such a complicated task on his own, especially since most of the time this occurs in the Scripture, a knowledge of future events would be necessary—events that had not happened at the time these men, chosen by God to author these biblical books, wrote them. Another reason would be so man could see woven in the Scripture the same plan of salvation for mankind that has been in place from the beginning, even before man's first sin.

*The First Melody*

To see this character displayed through the continued story line presented in God's interaction with Moses, I bring the attention to Moses's conversation with God after he's finished killing three thousand Israelites and wiping the blood from his sword. Remember from the last chapter, Moses realized he had not quite acted in accordance with the will of God when slaying these three thousand men. Not to ignore there is a wrath of God toward evil. There is! We will deal more with it later. Moses then sought to know the true character and ways of God. So, with this in mind, Moses made the long hike back up to the mountaintop and fasted again for another forty days, "seeking the LORD." He prayed to the LORD and asked God to show Him His ways so He can know Him.

> **Now therefore, I pray You, if I have found favor in Your sight, let me know Your ways that I may know You, so that I may find favor in Your sight. Consider too, that this nation is Your people." (Exodus 33:13 NASB)**

Is there a reason he's now seeking God's will? I believe there is. It's because He wants God's favor. God has just made clear to Moses he had just made a "minor" miscalculation (I'm being sarcastic) when acting on God's behalf, resulting in the death of three thousand brothers, sisters, and neighbors. Oh yeah, of the very people God was sending him to save from the cruel Egyptians. If I were Moses, I might be a little nervous. Remember, the only father figures we know that Moses had were the Pharaoh and the Egyptian taskmasters. God's gracious nature was aware of this as He responded to Moses. In **verse 17**, the LORD agreed to grant Moses's request.

> **The Lord said to Moses, "I will also do this thing of which you have spoken; for you have found favor in My sight and I have known you by name." (Exodus 33:17 NASB)**

Now then, Moses asked the LORD to show him His glory in **verse 18**. These words indicate that Moses is seeking a deeper, heavier, more intimate presence with God. It's almost as if he is asking for a "put me inside of you" type of closeness. Moses's heart is pure; his behavioral patterns and methods are flawed. If we are true, born-again believers, then our hearts desire to please Him and be like Him. However, our behavior patterns and methods of reacting to relational circumstances are so damaged. Remember, we learned our methods of coping with the fallen world before God's awareness and truth began its transforming work in us. Our pain from rejection, fear, physical and/or emotional abuse, and all the other negative aspects of the fallen world shaped our behavior patterns, while we were still in the fallen, sin-ruled condition. God responds.

> **And He said, "I Myself will make all My goodness pass before you, and will proclaim the name of the Lord before you; and I will be gracious to whom I will be gracious, and will show compassion on whom I will show compassion." (Exodus 33:19 NASB)**

God reminds Moses of two things about His nature. God alone is sovereign, with authority to issue judgment on a man's life and soul. And two, God's character is that of a good, gracious, and compassionate God. Using the Hebrew meanings of the words used in this verse, please allow me to paraphrase this passage so we can have a more complete understanding of it: "I will make My beauty, gladness, and joy cross over in front to cover you. I will proclaim and publish My renowned character of the Self-existent Creator to you. I will be fair and merciful and have pity on whom I choose, and I will love, fondle, and have compassion on whom I choose." God is in the process of answering Moses's prayer to show him His character as he asked in **Exodus 33:13**.

In the context of Moses's programming of his past, this comment from the all-powerful God must have really caught him by surprise. I know it would me. Most of all his life, Moses must have witnessed the Pharaoh and all other people in places of power and authority exercise a "ruling over with an iron hand, crushing under your feet" type of authoritative control. Rule by fear! The human race has been exposed to this type of controlling rule throughout time. Think about history, military rulers, kings, presidents, generals, the examples in movies, etc.

I still like the scenes in *The Equalizer* in which Denzel Washington woops up on all those evil men who used violent power over their underlings and victims to profit from organized crime. Or Liam Neeson in *Taken*. Superior good violence to conquer evil violence! The movie *Patton* is another example of this type of military-type control. We are surrounded and bombarded by this programming every day. Moses was just responding to the Israelite revelry event acting out what He believed God would've wanted him to do. Moses came down the mountain with the "Ten Commandments" written with the "finger of God." Seeing all these people engaged in evil revelry (partying and orgies) and possibly (likely) human sacrificing, he would have definitely felt the "righteous rage" of Denzel.

God's initial response to Moses was "I alone have the authority to punish, and I am compassionate and <u>gracious, slow to anger</u>, and abounding in lovingkindness and truth, who keeps lovingkindness for thousands, who forgives iniquity, transgression and sin…" God gave this basic understanding of His nature twice, both in this passage in **Exodus 33** and again in chapter 34. Imagine how different God's actual response is from what Moses might have expected from the all-powerful God of all creation in these circumstances!

> **But He said, "You cannot see My face, for no man can see Me and live!"**
> **Then the Lord said, "Behold, there is a place by Me, and you shall stand there on the rock; and it will come about, while My glory is passing by, that I will put you in the cleft of the rock and cover you with My hand until I have passed by.**

**Then I will take My hand away and you shall see My back, but My face shall not be seen." (Exodus 33:20–23 NASB)**

God tells Moses that His full presence is too powerful for frail mankind to live within proximity. It also may be saying that man, in his sinful imperfect condition, would immediately die in the presence of a pure and holy God, due to the fact that God's character is so pure that He cannot live with sin. This is one likely reason that Satan and all the angels who rebelled were cast out from God's presence in heaven. God's will appears to be that their destruction would not be immediate but rather delayed for a time to fulfill a purpose.

In any case, God allowed Moses to see all that was possible of His presence at this time. He places Moses in a crack or crevice in the rock for protection. He places his hand over him, again to shield and protect him from God's own incredible radiant presence, then passes His full face past Moses. Then God removes His hand and allows Moses to witness the presence of His train, or trailing glory. Maybe much like the trail of a comet. This is the first melody that God played in this dual symphonic display of **His omniscience**. Now the second.

*The Second Melody*

This particular melody requires a detailed review of Hebrew word meanings and scriptural interaction as a whole. In **verse 21** when God says, "There is a place by me and you shall stand," the word for "place" is "me qomah," which can mean both a place of locality and a condition of body and mind. It is from the root word "quwm," which means to abide, strengthen, make good, lift up, and raise up. The next word to review is "by," which simply means "with." The next word is that for "stand"; this word is "natsab," which means to appoint, erect, establish, rear upright, stand, and best state.

If we put this together, then this passage can also mean "There is a condition of body and mind that is with Me, inside Me where you will be lifted up, strengthened, and made good. You will be appointed and raised up to your best state of being on the rock" (paraphrased).

Now look at the word for "rock." This word is "tsuwr," and it means sharp rock, stone, and also **(mighty) God!** There are many scriptural references to the subject of a "rock." When you follow those references, you begin to see a pattern of its use in both Old and New Testament passages. Many of the passages refer to place of safety, protection, and refuge from various sorts of potential physical harm. Physical harm can be from the environment such as heat, flood, hail, and wind. Physical harm can be from military, war and weapons, etc. There are also many passages that use the term "rock" as a reference to God, or God's protection.

> **The Lord is my rock and my fortress and my deliverer, My God, my rock, in whom I take refuge; My shield and the horn of my salvation, my stronghold. (Psalm 18:2 NASB)**

> **For who is God, but the Lord? And who is a rock, except our God. (Psalm 18:31 NASB)**

> **The Lord lives, and blessed be my rock; And exalted be the God of my salvation. (Psalm 18:46 NASB)**

> **My soul, wait in silence for God only, For my hope is from Him.**
> **He only is my rock and my salvation, My stronghold; I shall not be shaken.**
> **On God my salvation and my glory rest; The rock of my strength, my refuge is in God. (Psalm 62:5–7 NASB)**

> **For in the day of trouble He will conceal me in His tabernacle; In the secret place of His tent He will hide me; He will lift me up on a rock. (Psalm 27:5 NASB)**

These Old Testament verses repeat the theme of Jehovah God or YHWH being our shielded place of safety, unmovable, predictably solid, and secure. In His presence come promises of safety from trouble, both physically and spiritually. The writers of the New Testament provide additional connection to this meaning.

> For I do not want you to be unaware, brethren, that our fathers were all under the cloud and all passed through the sea;
> and all were baptized into Moses in the cloud and in the sea;
> and all ate the same spiritual food;
> and all drank the same spiritual drink, for they were drinking from a spiritual rock which followed them; and the rock was Christ. (1 Corinthians 10:1–4 NASB)

This passage now makes a connection of God, Jehovah, YHWH, of the Old Testament to Jesus Christ! In addition, this passage links Jesus Christ to the events in the **exodus**. This "Rock" was the one that followed them in the desert as a fire by day and a cloud by night, providing guidance during the day and protection from the pursuing Egyptians during the night. Moses struck the rock to bring forth water for life sustenance when the Israelites were near death from dehydration having no water in the heat of the desert. This verse makes a crystal clear connection that this "Rock" is "Jesus Christ"! So Jesus was and is the guide and protector from the physical elements that potentially could harm both the Israelites and us.

> **But He was pierced through for our transgressions, He was crushed for our iniquities;**
> **The chastening for our well-being fell upon Him, And by His scourging we are healed. (Isaiah 53:5 NASB)**

> **For dogs have surrounded me; A band of evildoers has encompassed me; They pierced my hands and my feet. (Psalm 22:16 NASB)**

> **My God, my God, why have You forsaken me? Far from my deliverance are the words of my groaning. (Psalm 22:1 NASB)**

Both **Isaiah 53** and **Psalm 22** are prophetic scriptures that speak about Christ's coming crucifixion, Jesus being sacrificed for our sin to pay our death penalty. As always, God is more concerned with our "spiritual condition" more so than the physical condition. Not to say He doesn't care about our physical condition. He absolutely does. Recorded in the Scripture throughout is His attention to our health and mental well-being. He loves us. However, the eternal soul and spiritual well-being is so much more valuable because it is "eternal" and what provides us the ability to relate to Him and other fellow man. So here, these prophetic passages connect the idea that Jesus Christ was "pierced" for our sin, describing the type of death Jesus Christ was to endure, a crucifixion. The crucifixion details that His hands and feet were nailed or "pierced" to the cross. There's still yet more.

> **He made Him who knew no sin to be sin on our behalf, so that we might become the righteousness of God in Him. (2 Corinthians 5:21 NASB)**

Christ's sacrifice somehow makes it possible for us to become the "righteousness of God." This verse blows my mind. Almost makes me yell SACRILEGE or HERESY! Blasphemy! How can we even think anything about being "righteous"? Not to mention a righteous condition good enough to be spoken in the same sense as God's righteousness! For our body and mind to be brought to a condition of strength and goodness and to be raised up to our "best state" of being had something to do with being inside God on a rock called "Christ."

### Then Moses said, "I pray You, show me Your glory!" (Exodus 33:18 NASB)

Remember what Moses asked of God in **Exodus 33:18**? Moses asks the LORD to "show" him His glory. The word "show" is an action verb asking for God to provide Moses the ability to inspect, have a deep observation, perceive, have vision and insight, discern, distinguish, gaze intently, and study to the point of being able to duplicate. The word "glory" is more than splendor, honor, and reverence as we think of in the English translation or use of the word. In the Hebrew, this word also means "the dignity, reputation, abundance of what makes worthy." The root word means "to have weight, to be heavy, abundant." When put together, Moses appears to be asking God to reveal the deepest nature and character of God to him. Essentially to know the inside of His being that makes Him worthy of splendor and honor. It seems to indicate that Moses is seeking a deeper, heavier, more intimate presence with God. It's almost an asking for a "put me inside you" type of closeness so he can become the same nature and character as that of God the Father.

### In that day you will know that I am in My Father, and you in Me, and I in you. (John 14:20 NASB)

Connecting the event in **Exodus** of Moses's life gives this verse in **John 14:20** a much richer, deeper meaning. God was answering Moses's request when He let His glory pass by Moses. And He is answering the cry of our hearts as well through what He has done and is doing through Christ. Christ in us, He has become our righteousness. The righteousness of God!

### But He said, "You cannot see My face, for no man can see Me and live!"
### Then the Lord said, "Behold, there is a place by Me, and you shall stand there on the rock;

**and it will come about, while My glory is passing by, that I will put you in the cleft of the rock and cover you with My hand until I have passed by. (Exodus 33:20–22 NASB)**

The word for "**cleft**" of the rock is "ne qarah," which is a fissure, clift. It is from the root word "naqar," meaning to bore, pierce, put (thrust) out! Looking again at **Corinthians 5:21**, how does this word meaning line up with the one in **Exodus 33:22**? The **Rock**, Christ, was "pierced for our sin" and cast out of God the Father's presence when He took our sin upon Himself. When Jesus was dying on the cross and cried out, "My God, My God, why hast thou forsaken Me," He was for the first time in all of eternity separated, "cast out" from the presence of God the Father because he had taken our sin upon Himself, in effect becoming sin. This is written in **2 Corinthians 5:21**. His death enabled us to be made clean, and good, in God's presence and also made it possible for us to be placed inside the cleft (pierced place) of Christ (God). Jesus told His disciples that they would be "in" Him in **John 14:20**. One last verse to this second melody is in **verse 23**.

**Then I will take My hand away, and thou shalt see My back; but My face shall not be seen. (Exodus 33:23 NASB)**

I want to bring your attention to the word "hand." This is the Hebrew word "kaph," which describes the palm side of the hand in a cupped or curved position. This is a position of the hand used to hold, cradle, or cover something or someone. An act of protection. This same word can also mean a palm tree branch. In the Middle East region and in Hebrew tradition, a palm branch is a symbol of victory. Because of what Christ has done, we can now **stand victorious** inside Him (the Rock).

**After these things I looked, and behold, a great multitude which no one could count,**

**from every nation and all tribes and peoples and tongues, standing before the throne and before the Lamb, clothed in white robes, and palm branches were in their hands. (Revelation 7:9 NASB)**

In summary, the short version of the second melody, the "remez" (the hidden message), is this: *Because you have sin in you, My brightness and purity is so intense it is impossible to live in My presence! There is a condition of body and mind that is inside Me, because of Me, where you can be appointed and made upright, good, and achieve your fullest potential. I will hide you in My son, Jesus Christ, the "Rock," who will be pierced and cast out of my presence because He will take your sin upon Himself and die on your behalf to save you. I will cover you from My own powerful intensity and brightness in the pierced place of the Rock. When it has passed by, I will remove My protective loving hand from you and will declare you victorious.*

God has always had the same plan for salvation of mankind. And He does have a purpose, including the reason He cast Satan and his demons from heaven to earth to live a short time rather than recompense immediate destruction. God is, and has always been, revealing His nature and character to mankind. He is teaching us about subjects such as life, His love, sin, and its destruction. These truths are only hidden from those who will not accept Him and therefore will perish. **God is omniscient,** and He inspired the Scripture with certain words that often have dual meanings so that we would know that the Bible truly is God's Word and not just a work of literature from the hand of man. By the way, this passage in **Exodus** was written approximately one thousand five hundred years before Jesus Christ was born.

Remember that God's character qualities as told to Moses in **verse 19** are only able to be realized in your own life if you are hidden in the "Rock," Jesus Christ. Inside Jesus Christ, we are the "righteousness of God," fully redeemed, made new, made clean, and blameless. When He looks on us (believers), He only sees Christ's love covering us with His blood. There no longer remains anything to cause us to be cast out from His presence, or the life He planned from the beginning for us. Goodness means **gladness**, beauty, **joy**. Isn't this what we spend our whole life searching for? If you do not know Christ, then ask Him to come and live in you so that His power can begin the new life process.

# MOSES'S TESTING

MOSES WAS EIGHTY YEARS OLD when he was formally introduced to YHWH. From the evidence I have studied, he was an angry Hebrew man, rejected by both his own people and the Egyptian family he knew most. I would imagine very often, a child of a divorce might often feel a similar type of emotion. God the Father took him in, loved, nurtured, and made Moses feel valuable and important and taught him His true character. Moses has been seeking the LORD with all of his heart for a couple of years now.

We have studied Moses's anger and have seen it in action on a few occasions as outlined in the Scripture. During the last couple of years Moses has been walking with the LORD, things really haven't been all that smooth. Just about the time you think things are getting better, something else seems to unravel our pursuit of paradise plans. We get tested. Happens to all of us. Why? What's God doing? Why is this repetitive pattern so necessary? We're going to look at this issue in this chapter. Moses will get tested. How will Moses stand the test of a rebellion against his authority (which was God given) from the people? Will Moses again take the sword of divine judgment, or has Moses learned something new from walking with God the Father?

The setting takes place in the wilderness where Moses and the Israelites have been wandering since they left Egypt. I've seen this "wilderness." Growing up, reading the Exodus account in the Bible, I imagined it must have looked like a forest near where I lived. Wide-open acreages of forest trees and years of layered decaying leaves on the forest floor. The smell of fall, and a damp musty forest air mingled with a clean oxygen-enriched air. I would hear animals scurrying through the leaves, escaping my presence as they heard me coming. Not a house or street in sight—for miles. You definitely could get turned around and lost, although probably not for forty years. The "wilderness"!

Then I took a dive trip to the Red Sea and saw from a plane this "wilderness" as it really was. At first, I didn't think about the Israelites, Moses, or the exodus. My first thought, as I looked out the window down at the terrain was *Wow, what is that?* There were black barren hills of rock and sand. No vegetation of any kind, at least not that you could see from the air. It was not just rock and sand, but a dark black/grey color. The color that attracts and radiates heat. Imagine the hottest desert on the planet! When I realized it was a barren, hot desert that seemed to stretch on for eternity, my thoughts began to run survival probabilities should I find myself down there lost. As the flight time grew longer, seeing how vast this wide-open barren hellhole was, I determined my survival chances were not good! More like zero! After seeing hundreds of miles of this totally barren and lifeless dark sandpit, I then thought about Moses and the Israelites. I wondered how they got out at all, much less being lost for only forty years. Not kidding!

This is the "wilderness" setting for the event in this chapter. During the second year after they left Egypt, God presented Moses and the Israelites an opportunity to enter "the promised land." The spies were sent, to view this land God was offering them, and they brought back the report. It was a green, pristine, fruitful paradise! The first view of the land was most likely at Jericho, a city of palm trees located on a beautiful stretch of the Jordan River. The river valley was lush and green with a backdrop of beautiful multicolored cliff walls. The climate and rich soil conditions brought by the spring-fed Jordan River made it possible to grow the best fruit and crops of every kind. Grape clusters were so big they had to carry them back on a pole supported by two men. This land "flowing with milk and honey" was a stark contrast to the hot, desert wilderness they had been roaming in for the last year or two!

However, the spies returned with a negative report. They reported about how fortified the cities were and how large the people of the land were. Only two of the twelve spies trusted God's word that "He would go before them and give the enemy into their hands."

The other ten spies were fearful of the inhabitants. Therefore, those ten along with all the people voted against seizing the land. They were content to trust only in their <u>own</u> ability and thus satisfied to wander in that wonderful "wilderness" desert. Who does that?

Before I approach the subject of the test Moses is about to undergo, as mentioned in the opening paragraphs, allow me to digress a moment. Here is another event that happens along the way. One day, an Israelite started gathering wood on the Sabbath. It seems harmless enough. What was the big deal? Certainly it was not an offense punishable by death! The man was brought to Moses. The LORD instructed that the man be stoned to death outside the camp. This they did.

> Now while the sons of Israel were in the wilderness, they found a man gathering wood on the sabbath day.
>
> Those who found him gathering wood brought him to Moses and Aaron and to all the congregation;
>
> and they put him in custody because it had not been declared what should be done to him. Then the Lord said to Moses, "The man shall surely be put to death; all the congregation shall stone him with stones outside the camp."
>
> So all the congregation brought him outside the camp and stoned him to death with stones, just as the Lord had commanded Moses. (Numbers 15:32–36 NASB)
>
> Remember the sabbath day, to keep it holy. (Exodus 20:8 NASB)
>
> Therefore you are to observe the sabbath, for it is holy to you. Everyone who profanes it shall surely be put to death; for whoever does

**any work on it, that person shall be cut off from among his people. (Exodus 31:14 NASB)**

**You shall work six days, but on the seventh day you shall rest;** *even* **during plowing time and harvest you shall rest. (Exodus 34:21 NASB)**

**You shall not kindle a fire in any of your dwellings on the sabbath day. (Exodus 35:3 NASB)**

**If because of the sabbath you turn your foot from doing your own pleasure on My holy day, and call the sabbath a delight, the holy day of the LORD honorable, and shall honor it, desisting from your own ways, from seeking your own pleasure, and speaking your own word,**
**Then you will take delight in the LORD and I will make you ride on the heights of the earth; and I will feed you with the heritage of Jacob your father, for the mouth of the LORD has spoken. (Isaiah 58:13–14 NASB)**

To make sense of why God instructed this, allow me to explain the symbolism of the Sabbath and the camp. This man was trying to sustain life (i.e., gathering the wood) by gathering provision to cook, stay warm, see at night, etc., rather than trusting by faith in God for his provision. The "Sabbath" represents the entering into the eternal rest of God (**Hebrews 3:7–4:16**). This is only possible through the atoning shed blood of Christ. We die to self (dying to sustaining life by self-effort) and become reborn into the life of Christ by faith through His life-sustaining sacrifice.

Thus, working on the Sabbath is a man-made futile attempt to experience an abundant life the way God intended from the beginning. Since life comes from God, in essence, it is attempting to work your way into God's favor (eternal rest, life) by good deeds such as church contributions, going to church every time the door is open, being a member of the choir, learning eloquent prayers, etc. If finding God's favor isn't high on your priority list, then the other purpose for working on the Sabbath is an attempt to find this abundant life by some self-ordained method other than the way the Creator designed. Abundant life without God. What an absurd thought, since God is the Creator and sustainer of life!

The camp of course symbolizes the body of Christ, the church! The equivalent in Moses's day are the Israelite people who surrounded the tabernacle waiting to enter into the holy of holies (heaven)! God was simply expressing that in His plan, anyone attempting to earn their own way into eternal rest (heaven) or find true life in any way other than His designed plan would be outside of the body of Christ (His true church). Therefore, the result would be eternal death of the soul. Then the LORD commanded Moses to have the people make robes with tassels on the fringe to serve as a reminder of all the commandments.

> **It shall be a tassel for you to look at and remember all the commandments of the LORD, so as to do them and not follow after your own heart and your own eyes, after which you played the harlot. (Numbers 15:39 NASB; emphasis mine)**

The LORD hit the nail on the head in this passage. True quality life is found in living by faith as God designed it, not in ways governed by your own thinking and understanding. He laid it out for us in God's word. With this in mind, look at one the first major tests of Moses's spiritual growth he has learned the last couple of years.

### Korah's Rebellion

Immediately following this event, Korah, a Levite, along with men named Dathan and Abiram (Reubenites), rose up to challenge Moses's authority. They came up along with 250 leaders of the Israelite congregation. This was not a spur-of-the-moment uprising.

This was an organized coup. To organize 250 supporters, especially those men who were considered tribal leaders, "men of renown," is evidence that this uprising had been brewing throughout the camp for quite a while.

These tribal leaders, "men of renown," are the popular elite of society. Today's equivalent are our Hollywood elite, political leaders, and cultural influential icons of society. They are most often the most wealthy and powerful of society who have attained the highest form of life known to man outside of God. That doesn't make them god-less, just because they are wealthy and influential. There are many people who truly worship the one, true Almighty God who happens to have wealth and/or influence. However, by and large, the majority of those in this arena find no need to worship God because their lux-urious lifestyle fills their emptiness just enough to trust in it for life. These are the ones of whom Jesus spoke when he said in **Luke 18:25 (NASB), "For it is easier for a camel to go through the eye of a needle than for a rich man to enter into the kingdom of God."** Essentially this sets a dividing line between worshippers of God and worshippers of self as god, or humanism.

It appears that this event with the man gathering wood on the Sabbath may have been the catalyst that ignited the confrontation with Moses. We can only speculate as to why, but their main com-plaints indicated that they might have thought the rules of Moses's religion might be too harsh or unfair. Their main complaint was expressed in **Numbers 16:3 (NASB).**

> And they assembled themselves together against Moses and Aaron, and said unto them, "You have gone far enough, for all the congrega-tion are holy, every one of them, and the LORD is in their midst; so why do you exalt yourselves above the assembly of the LORD?"

Their claim was "all the congregation are holy" and the LORD is with each one equally. Then they accused Moses of exalting himself to a position of authority. This is a modern-day example of a power grab, where those seeking absolute power make promises of some sort to others in order to gain their support. Moses suspects they didn't get their authority from God. Moses knew he resisted accepting responsibility of authority over the Israelites with everything he had, yet God insisted upon placing him in that position. Moses also knew that the people were not holy but that only those who were anointed and cleansed for service were presented as holy for service to God (see **Jude 5; 1 Corinthians 10:2–10**). In other words, Korah's theology was flawed, and he was acting under a self-appointed authority. Yet no doubt Moses was facing a hostile group of a significant number.

I might have thought, *Where's my sword?* However, that thought again puts my own flawed belief of God the Father's character on display. Please allow me to point out another possibility. Korah was a Levite. Was he one of those who came to join Moses in his religious zeal for judging everyone his neighbor and everyone his brother with the sword on the day three thousand were killed? Was it possible that Moses himself, in his sin, taught Korah that having absolute power was all that mattered in controlling the people? Use good violence to defeat evil violence, like in the movies!

Korah may also have learned if you controlled their religion, you could control the people. Or maybe Korah harbored anger over the loss and grief of a loved one during that incident of Moses's unrighteous zeal, causing him to resent Moses? Could this now be part of the reaping of Moses's earlier sin he had sowed? We cannot be sure, but other scripture may indicate this possibility. I'll write more detail about this later.

> **When Moses heard this, he fell on his face; and he spoke to Korah and all his company, saying, "Tomorrow morning the Lord will show who is His, and who is holy, and will bring him near to Himself; even the one whom He will choose, He will bring near to Himself.**
>
> **Do this: take censers for yourselves, Korah and all your company, and put fire in them, and lay incense upon them in the**

> **presence of the Lord tomorrow; and the man whom the Lord chooses shall be the one who is holy. You have gone far enough, you sons of Levi!" (Numbers 16:4–7 NASB)**

> **Another angel came and stood at the altar, holding a golden censer; and much incense was given to him, so that he might add it to the prayers of all the saints on the golden altar which was before the throne.**
> **And the smoke of the incense, with the prayers of the saints, went up before God out of the angel's hand. (Revelation 8:3–4 NASB)**

This verse makes clear what the incense represented. It is the prayers of those that belong to the LORD. Moses bows low before Korah, humbling himself before Korah and God. Moses appears to have learned from the LORD, through the earlier events, that he was not without sin himself. Therefore, Moses did not believe he was in a position to throw rocks or judge Korah in spite of Korah's own misguided thinking. This time he was not about to assume knowing God's intentions or methods of action. Moses asks Korah to return to the LORD "in prayer and supplication" (censers of incense) all night and return in the morning. If he still felt the same about the authority issue, then Moses claimed that the LORD would choose for Himself who is holy.

In **Numbers 16:8–11,** Moses reminded them that the LORD had already assigned the prestigious and holy task of service of the tabernacle, as well as the duty to minister to the congregation. However, Korah and his merry men had their hearts set on the priesthood instead. They may have recognized the power the priesthood held. Much like the judicial branch of today, it held power to interpret the law. The only difference is that the priesthood of that day also made the laws, enforced the laws, controlled the tithes, and all other aspects of social life as well! In comparison to the United States form of government, the priesthood held the power of all three branches of government as well as the social responsibility of the church: the executive, legislative, and judicial. This may have been an appealing position Korah envied to have. He might have thought he could make better judgments or be a better leader or better priest than Moses.

In love, God tried to warn Korah, Dathan, and Abiram of their fatal flaw just before they carried it out. Instead of looking inward to self-examination and repentance, they responded with anger and rebellion. Moses urged Dathan and Abiram to come up also and take censers and burn incense before the Lord. This meant for them "to pray over the matter before the Lord all night." They not only refused, but they threw up one of their favorite complaints. It's spoken in Numbers 16:13–14 (NASB).

> **Is it not enough that you have brought us up out of a land flowing with milk and honey to have us die in the wilderness, but you would also lord it over us?**
>
> **Indeed, you have not brought us into a land flowing with milk and honey, nor have you given us an inheritance of fields and vineyards. Would you put out the eyes of these men? We will not come up!"**

It appears their recollection of Egypt was somewhat different from the reality of how it really was. Even though Egypt was a land flowing with milk and honey, the Israelites were not allowed to have any of it! It was really more desert and hardship than they might remember. They forgot that they were **slaves** in Egypt. God brought them out of Egypt and within eighteen months took them straight to the promised land and told them to take it. That He had given it into their hands. It was the Israelites' own choice not to trust the Lord God and to not enter it! Moses tried to reason with them by asking them to seek the Lord. Their hearts were hard.

We are the same today as well. We can easily become angry or disenchanted with something or someone. I've experienced it in work, ministry, recreation, family events, etc. "I should be the one selected to sing that solo." "I know more about that subject than that preacher." "I could've done that seminar with more enthusiasm." "Why is she making all the family decisions?" Our memory of facts and events becomes somewhat skewed or distorted from the truth when we are unhappy or disgruntled. An examination of our partisan government of today reveals this quite well. This is natural human tendency. It takes a concerted effort within the power of the Holy Spirit to control our emotions well enough to not distort the facts. Yet it is necessary for good judgment.

> **Then the LORD spoke to Moses and Aaron, saying, "Separate yourselves from among this congregation, that I may consume them instantly." But they fell on their faces and said, "O God, God of the spirits of all flesh, when one man sins, will You be angry with the entire congregation?"**
>
> **Then the LORD spoke to Moses, saying, "Speak to the congregation, saying, 'Get back from around the dwellings of Korah, Dathan and Abiram.'" (Numbers 16: 20–24 NASB)**

Here comes the showdown. As they approached the tent of meeting with their censers, they were ready for a fight! The glory of the LORD begins to appear. The LORD tells Moses to "separate yourselves from the families and supporters of Korah, Dathan, and Abiram so He could consume them instantly"! Moses interceded on behalf of the congregation and pleaded for only the leaders of the rebellion to be held accountable for the sin, and not the whole congregation. The LORD then called the people to separate to either the side of Korah (rebellion) or the side of Moses (righteousness by faith). If they believed Moses and separated themselves from the households of Korah, Dathan, and Abiram, and their followers, then they would be spared. If they didn't believe Him, then this would be considered an act of rebellion against God.

Anyone with an ounce of common sense would have obeyed Moses and separated themselves from Korah, Dathan, and Abiram, especially in light of all the miracles that seemed to come from Moses's hand. What mighty miracles of God had they witnessed through the hand of Korah lately? Even if you didn't agree with or understand Moses on all the issues, with the track record he had, why take a chance? So some of the people got back from around Korah, Dathan, and Abiram.

**And Moses said, "By this you shall know that the LORD has sent me to do all these deeds; for this is not my doing.**

**If these men die the death of all men, or if they suffer the fate of all men; then the LORD has not sent me.**

**But if the LORD brings about an entirely new thing, and the ground opens its mouth and swallows them up, with all that is theirs, and they descend alive into Sheol; then you will understand that these men have spurned the LORD." (Numbers 16:28–30 NASB)**

Moses has passed this test in learning more of God's ways. In the golden calf event, Moses took judgment in his own hands and executed what he thought was God's will, killing three thousand of the people. This time Moses completely trusted God alone with the discipline or judgment of the contentious men, as well as on himself. He was remembering God's word in **Exodus 32:34: "Nevertheless in the day when I punish, I will punish them for their sin."** And in **Hebrews 10:30: "For we know Him who said, 'Vengeance is mine, I will repay.'"** And again, **"The LORD will judge his people."**

This is what makes this next part so interesting. Moses predicted ahead of time how this rebellious group will be killed by extraordinary means. He said it would be by an earthquake. The scriptural reference **Numbers 16:31–34** details God's righteous judgment. As soon as Moses finished speaking, an earthquake occurred that was so powerful that it opened up the ground and swallowed these men, their families including their children, wives, and all their belongings!

The earthquake would've been spectacular enough; but its precision was so surgical that it only engulfed Korah, Dathan, Abiram, and their families. In addition to the precise earthquake, God provides an additional show of His power and support of Moses's authority by bringing a fire that consumed the other 250 supporters of this rebellion! Again, it was so precise that not another hair was singed on anyone except those 250 identified men! You might think that would've settled the issue. But men without God have no understanding.

**But on the next day all the congregation of the sons of Israel grumbled against Moses and Aaron, saying, "You are the ones who have caused the death of the Lord's people." (Numbers 16:41 NASB)**

I just have one word for this part, "unbelievable"! This is stupidity or ignorance at its finest! You would think that after this mighty display of God's precision-perfect power, using the earthquake and consuming fire, the people would certainly have gotten the message to leave Moses alone and not doubt his authority. Even if they doubted that God supported Moses and that Moses's own power was enough to bring about an earthquake without God (which he wasn't), then I don't think I would be bold enough to confront him. However, that's what they did! I can choose to disbelieve or disagree with someone or something, but I'm not an idiot. I have learned to keep my mouth shut and live to fight another day. Okay, Moses, you know the drill… God again warns Moses to "GET BACK!"

You see, God was right the first time when He was about to destroy the whole congregation. God already knew their heart. They were going to resist and rebel against the Almighty God to the death! Yet in order to teach Moses more about His ways, God listened and heard Moses's prayer to spare them. This was to show Moses that God does indeed hear and respond to our prayers. His character is compassionate and patient, slow to anger, not wanting any to perish. God also uses this response to Moses in these passages to teach us His ways. The scriptural reference **Numbers 16:46–48** provides Moses's response to God's warning. A plague begins to move throughout the camp. The plague is powerful enough to bring not just sickness but death!

> **Moses said to Aaron, "Take your censer and put in it fire from the altar, and lay incense on it; then bring it quickly to the congregation and make atonement for them, for wrath has gone forth from the Lord, the plague has begun!"**
>
> **Then Aaron took it as Moses had spoken, and ran into the midst of the assembly, for behold, the plague had begun among the people. So he put on the incense and made atonement for the people.**
>
> **He took his stand between the dead and the living, so that the plague was checked. (Numbers 16:46–48 NASB)**

Again, in contrast to Moses's earlier zeal, he now only had a compassionate heart for the people. To save as many as he could from God's consuming wrath! Moses instructed Aaron to run through the congregation with the censer of incense to make atonement on their behalf. He exercised intercessory prayer for the people. Isn't this what God was trying to teach Moses earlier? To take ownership of the people and teach them God's ways. To lead them to salvation. Moses didn't allow his own anger to overcome his compassionate heart. These people were lacking in understanding of God and His ways. Moses instead took the opportunity to love the people by intercession in prayer on their behalf to a pure and holy God. Aaron exercised intercessory prayer for the people. Today Jesus intercedes on our behalf. He is the bridge between sinful man and our Holy Father. Jesus prays for us.

In recalling the people's response to the twelve spies' report, the people chose not to enter into the promised land God had given into their hand. All they had to do was to trust Him to go before them as He said He would. Since they chose not to enter (to trust GOD), God then pronounced a sentence upon that generation of Israelites.

> **Surely all the men who have seen My glory and My signs which I performed in Egypt and in the wilderness, yet have put Me to the test these ten times and have not listened to My voice, shall by no means see the land which I swore to their fathers, nor shall any of those who spurned Me see it. (Numbers 14:22–23 NASB)**

> **How long shall I bear with this evil congregation who are grumbling against Me? I have heard the complaints of the sons of Israel, which they are making against Me.**
>
> **Say to them, "As I live," says the Lord, "just as you have spoken in My hearing, so I will surely do to you;**
>
> **your corpses will fall in this wilderness, even all your numbered men, according to your complete number from twenty years old and upward, who have grumbled against Me.**
>
> **Surely you shall not come into the land in which I swore to settle you, except Caleb the son of Jephunneh and Joshua the son of Nun.**
>
> **Your children, however, whom you said would become a prey—I will bring them in, and they will know the land which you have rejected.**
>
> **But as for you, your corpses will fall in this wilderness.**
>
> **Your sons shall be shepherds for forty years in the wilderness, and they will suffer for**

**your unfaithfulness, until your corpses lie in
the wilderness." (Numbers 14:27–33 NASB)**

God was in the process of weeding out the hard-hearted, unbelieving people from the Israelite nation so that those who remained were of a soft heart of clay (the faithful). These could finally be given rest in the promised land. God knew this generation would never learn to trust Him to find the only true life. The longer it took to weed out these evil-hearted men, the longer it would be before the faithful could finally enter into their inheritance. When all the acts of the play are ended, what often appears to be God's impatience or harshness ultimately displays that God's actions are always driven by a compassionate heart of love, mercy, and justice for all His chosen ones!

God's desire to allow the destruction of the whole congregation instead of just Korah and his men was just. This is because they chose to not serve and worship God! Their hearts were so blinded by their rebellion against worshipping Him to the point of losing all common sense. To ignore blatant facts such as the miracles through the hand of Moses, parting the Red Sea, obtaining water from the rock, the earthquake, etc., and still choose to rebel against Moses as the chosen representative of God borders on insanity. It ends in death, eternally, not just physical death on this earth. God already knew the hardened heart would never submit to Him. Judgment sentencing was passed. God showed His patient heart in giving the congregation an extended offer to repent of the rebellion. They became even more hardened. The final sentence was passed.

Moses was successful in learning from God a different way of life. He was moved from being an angry (emotional), legalistic person with a harsh judgmental attitude toward those trapped by sin to a patient, humble, loving person with an intercessory approach to those trapped by sin. He learned to allow God, the **only true righteous judge**, to issue discipline and judgment upon others. Korah, Dathan, and Abiram did not know God's ways and were attempting to establish their own way to life and/or God through their own limited thinking and reasoning.

This attempt to find life/salvation through any method other than Christ is direct rebellion against God and His sole plan of salvation. The phrase Korah used when he said, "All the congregation are holy," is another version of "All roads lead to Rome." In religious terms, we hear it today as "All religions lead to God." I'm sorry, but believing this lie will lead to certain death!

In the last chapter, God's omniscience was highlighted by the use of "pishot" and "remez." This is the simultaneous expression of a surface meaning or story line at the same time a hidden or second story line is being communicated through the writings in an underlying message. Here it is again. The event of the man gathering sticks on the Sabbath and the rebellion of Korah are not two separate incidents; they are connected together as one story in the account of the exodus. They are both forms of rebellion. One is against God's instruction regarding the Sabbath; the other is what appeared to be against Moses's authority. In reality, they were both expressions of rebellion against God's authority and instruction to enter into abundant, eternal life. This is the core issue of life itself for all eternity past, present, and future! It's a choice.

The Scripture has written it in many places in the sixty-six books that make up the Bible. Joshua 24:15 says it this way, "Choose this day whom you will serve..." As mentioned earlier, this is the dividing line. Either a person will choose to worship, honor, and trust in the God of creation for life, or they will choose to resist, rebel, and refuse to worship "the only God" and insist on some kind of life without God. Another name for it is humanism, the form of worshipping the human self as god. It is the single most important decision one will ever make.

Stoning to death the man gathering sticks on the Sabbath seems harsh, or does it? You see, the man gathering sticks to make fire, cook, and provide warmth and sustenance for himself and his family on the Sabbath was a decision to find life without trusting God to supply it. The Sabbath represented the entering into the eternal day of rest where one who believes in God puts their trust in him to provide all that is necessary for that quality abundant life that never ends! God does all the work necessary to bring us into His provision of "the promised land." Our part is to believe in God's design for life.

We can't earn it. We only need to trust in Him to bring it all about. By this believing, we have entered into that final Sabbath day of rest that is without end. **The <u>evidence</u> of believing is the willingness to obey the instruction.** We obey and submit to His authority and design because we believe. The Sabbath day of rest. We will no longer fear death or lack. We are able to trust in God to provide and protect. This man rejected God's ordained design.

Korah's rebellion was the same "remez" message. Korah thought his own thinking in making decisions for life would result in a higher-quality life for himself and all the people. It's the same thinking of the "politically correct" elite who would make decisions on our behalf to provide the highest-quality life. However, it must reject the knowledge and submission to worship the One and Only true God of all creation and all that He instructed to find life! The "politically correct" thinking is based solely on man's limited and flawed thinking. It's a deception. The result will end the same as the man gathering sticks on the Sabbath. They will not enter into the Sabbath rest of the "promised land flowing with milk and honey." They will miss the highest-quality abundant life here on this earth, as well as the eternity of that quality life. The result of rebellion against God's design for life is death—eternally.

There is a wrath of God. It's not an anger that hates man. It's an anger that hates what the deception of sin does to man. He hates the fear, pain, and atrocious harm the sin brings to man's heart, mind, and body. The cruelty done to the most innocent (the children) of our society (i.e., physical, sexual, emotional, and verbal abuse). The evil acts on the humans He so dearly loves brought by a mind crazed with the deceptiveness of sin. The wrath of God is the simple understanding that His holiness and purity is so high and intense that His nature cannot live with sin. It must and will be destroyed forever. God is love; there can be no eternity that includes sin. It's an impossibility because His nature cannot dwell with it.

Humanism rejects the purity of a Holy God and allows for a continued fallen man condition ruled by sin. God's love was displayed in the precision judgment on those who would forever reject submitting to the worship of Him as God as He created it to be. This precision spared the people (or their offspring) who would become a believer covered by God's plan to enter into that eternal rest.

To us as believers, the incense represents the prayers of intercession for an unbelieving people around us. We are being instructed to pray on their behalf to save them from this deception of rebellious humanism. Being a god of your own life will result in death. Our prayers can prolong the life for what may at present appear to be an unbeliever. This may grant additional time or bring additional influence to provide more opportunity for them to come to a knowledge of the truth. Please don't take this lightly. The eternal quality of life of your children, grandchildren, friends, and loved ones around you may be in the balance.

# LIVING WATER

WATER. THEY KEEP LOOKING FOR it on the moon, Mars, planets both in our solar system and outside our solar system. The reason is obvious. Life cannot exist without it, at least not for very long. Man will die from lack of it within three days, give or take a few hours. A healthy human body consists of over 70–78 percent water. The creation story begins with it in **Genesis 1:2**, "And the Spirit of God was moving over the surface of the waters." The significance of it is paramount for life itself.

Water is this incredible universal solvent, "meaning that almost every substance can dissolve in water." It is also one of only a few materials that can exist as solid, liquid, and gas within a relatively narrow range of temperatures. It's a detergent that cleanses almost everything. It flows, therefore creating the perfect medium or condition to transport nutrients to feed cell life while carrying away waste toxins needed to maintain the healthy life growth cycle.

Water in vapor form or ice becomes a shield against radiation from the sun. Without its properties in the clouds, the earth's crust would burn up and turn to dust and rock. All life would die. It's a thermal blanket that holds moisture in (like a canopy), while reflecting radiation, and light away. It warms the body as well as cools the skin. Think of how a greenhouse feels. You envision heavy, thick, moist, and warm air creating the perfect environment to grow plant life and almost everything else.

We love water for recreational aesthetic properties. We flock to it on vacation. VRBO (Vacation Rental by Owner) or Airbnb (Air Bed-and-Breakfast) with a lake view, ocean view, river view, waterfalls, poolside, water slide, snow or water skiing, fishing, boating, etc. It's the perfect form of relaxation and a stress reliever. Tubs or pools of water help heal and soothe sore muscles and tensed nerves and calm the spirit. It's more than just a physical need and sensation to our health. Its properties reach deep into the soul as well. Most of us don't stop long enough to consider how important water is to us. And we certainly don't spend much time recognizing its effect on our soul. But it's there!

This brief reminder of the importance of water might help us better understand why Jesus referred to it often. He spoke to the woman at the well, "And He would have given you living water" (**John 4:10**) As He stood in the temple, He spoke, "From his innermost being will flow rivers of living water" (**John 7:38**). God the Father used it in the "wilderness" when sustaining life for the Israelites by supplying water that flowed from the rock. God uses elements of life we can understand to explain things we don't understand. He loves to teach and take time to nurture our heart of understanding. He loves to lead us into life. So what is the significance of this "living water"?

In the last chapter, the Scripture made it apparent Moses was progressing in his understanding of the LORD's ways. It seems he passed the test with Korah with flying colors. However, Moses knew to whom the credit belonged, to the LORD alone! I would like to shift the focus in this chapter to another test Moses faced near the end of his life. On this test, Moses did not fare as well. In fact, he failed this test miserably. I want to look at this failure, its consequences, and attempt to make an application of it to our own lives. More importantly, since this is a book about God the Father's character, let's look at how God dealt with and viewed this failure.

This test takes place toward the end of Moses's life. Moses is the youngest of his siblings, Aaron and Miriam. This event is preceded by the death of Miriam upon arriving at Kadesh in the Wilderness of Zin. The word "Kadesh" means "sanctuary, holy place, set apart for purpose, sanctified." Moses was still grieving the loss of his beloved sister at this place. Immediately prior to their arriving here, the LORD had just issued to them the ordinance of the red heifer (**Numbers 19:2–7**). The ordinance of the red heifer was an ordinance of purification for uncleanliness, which could arise when a person touched a corpse, grave, or human bone. The passage in **Numbers 19:17** established that this purification process required a vessel of "running or flowing" water as translated in most versions. This word is also translated as "living" water.

> **Then for the unclean person they shall take some of the ashes of the burnt purification from sin and flowing water shall be added to them in a vessel. (Numbers 19:17 NASB)**

> **Then the sons of Israel, the whole congregation, came to the wilderness of Zin in the first month; and the people stayed at Kadesh. Now Miriam died there and was buried there.**
> **There was no water for the congregation, and they assembled themselves against Moses and Aaron. (Numbers 20:1–2 NASB)**

As explained in **Numbers 20:1–2**, immediately following the death of Miriam, the congregation began to grumble again against Moses and Aaron because there was no water. Since Miriam had to be buried, it's possible that this event caused the people to begin looking for a water source in order to purify themselves. It's possible there was concern for the lack of water for the purification process, but if you believe this was the real reason for their grumbling, then I have some prime real estate to sell you in the everglades of Florida. Drinking water and water for all the other aesthetic and practical applications mentioned at the beginning of this chapter was the real concern.

When the Israelites would set out to move locations, they would have carried a water supply with them until they found camp. Whether or not that portable water supply was depleted is not clear. Under normal camping circumstances, my sons and I would hike until we found a suitable place to camp. A sufficient water source was a primary priority. Why would the Israelites just stop to camp without making sure it was a suitable location? Remember, they were experienced desert wilderness campers. They had been doing it for nearly forty years to this point. Did the LORD know they were without water? This passage should shed some light on these questions.

> **On the day the tabernacle, the Tent of the Testimony, was set up, the cloud covered it. From evening till morning the cloud above the tabernacle looked like fire.**
>
> **That is how it continued to be; the cloud covered it, and at night it looked like fire.**
>
> **Whenever the cloud lifted from above the Tent, the Israelites set out; wherever the cloud settled, the Israelites encamped.**
>
> **At the LORD's command the Israelites set out, and at His command they encamped. As long as the cloud stayed over the tabernacle, they remained in camp. (Numbers 9:15–18 NIV)**

Not only did the LORD know of their egregious condition, but it seems it was by His design. The LORD directed the path of the Israelites in the cloud by day and the pillar of fire by night. When the cloud lifted up from the tabernacle, they were to pack up and move. When it settled to the ground, they were to set up camp. The LORD was intimately involved in their day-to-day lives and circumstances. The LORD chose this dry campsite! What's up with that?

It was necessary for God to provide the living water for both the sustenance of life and the purification process. The Israelites' concern was not for spiritual righteousness, but for physical life sustenance. The LORD attempted to get the Israelites to trust Him for their provision. The LORD had tried to get them to learn this from Him on other occasions, but they had great difficulty learning to trust their faithful God. Therefore, they didn't trust in the LORD for their provision here either.

Moses and Aaron were focused more on grieving the loss of their sister. Their focus was on the spiritual, the hereafter. The Israelites' grumbling for thirst (if indeed it was that bad) seemed pale in comparison to the anguish of their thoughts of Miriam's passing. Moses and Aaron, to say the least, were upset about their lack of sensitivity.

They followed with their usual complaints about how Egypt was better, how they had not seen a land "flowing with milk and honey," and how they wished they would have died in the plagues of Korah, Abiram, and Dathan. Blah, blah, blah, as they say. I'm sure at this point Moses and Aaron wished they would have died too. They were probably second-guessing their willingness to intercede on their behalf before the LORD, to spare them. Have you ever met anyone like these Israelites? I have. I don't like to admit it, but I'm like that at times too. The truth is, we all are.

> **And the Lord spoke to Moses, saying, "Take the rod; and you and your brother Aaron assemble the congregation and speak to the rock before their eyes, that it may yield its water. You shall thus bring forth water for them out of the rock and let the congregation and their beasts drink." (Numbers 20:7–8 NASB)**

Since the LORD was keenly aware of the Israelites' need (and it was a legitimate need), He was just waiting for the people to ask for it (**James 4:2–3**). How often do we get angry and start grumbling about our circumstances or needs before we ever go to the LORD and simply ask? Moses and Aaron again fell prostrate at the door of the tabernacle to plead with the Lord for help. At this point, let me remind you this was the second time the people were in need of water. The first time, the LORD provided water from a rock, it occurred at Rephidim in the Wilderness of Sin (**Exodus 17:1–7**).

The first time the LORD commanded Moses to strike the rock and it gushed forth water. This time, however, God commanded Moses to speak to the rock in the presence of the people for their water. Why this difference? To get a clear understanding of this, Scripture research is needed to find the symbolic meaning of some key components of these accounts. From previous chapters, we have learned that the rock is symbolic of Christ.

> **For I do not want you to be ignorant of the fact, brothers and sisters, that our ancestors were all under the cloud and that they all passed through the sea.**
>
> **They were all baptized into Moses in the cloud and in the sea.**
>
> **They all ate the same spiritual food and drank the same spiritual drink; for they drank from the spiritual rock that accompanied them, and that rock was Christ. (1 Corinthians 10:1–4 NASB)**

If the rock is Christ, what is the significance of striking it to bring forth water? Before we clarify this, look at another symbolism in God's Word: the water.

> **But whoever drinks of the water that I will give him shall never thirst; but the water that I will give him will become in him a well of water springing up to eternal life. (John 4:14 NASB)**

> **Now on the last day, the great day of the feast, Jesus stood and cried out, saying, "If anyone is thirsty, let him come to Me and drink.**
>
> **He who believes in Me, as the Scripture said, 'From his innermost being will flow rivers of living water.'"**
>
> **But this He spoke of the Spirit, whom those who believed in Him were to receive; for the Spirit was not yet given, because Jesus was not yet glorified. (John 7:37–39 NASB)**

> **But I tell you the truth: It is for your good that I am going away. Unless I go away, the Counselor will not come to you; but if I go, I will send him to you. (John 16:7 NIV)**

This verse when read in its entire context makes it clear to us that the Counselor refers to the Holy Spirit. The Greek word used also means "to come alongside to help; or intercessor." This verse helps us understand that Christ had to go away (ascend) before the Holy Spirit could enter into His chosen believers. We now know that the rock is Christ, and the water represents the Holy Spirit that Christ places in all born-again believers who are a new creation in Him. So to put it all together, this is a prophecy in the Pentateuch, of Christ (the Rock) being struck down (crucified); and as a result, Living Water (the Holy Spirit) gushed forth, giving life to all who would drink it (accept Him as Savior). However, why is Moses being tested again to provide water for the people? They are still in the Wilderness of Zin. What is the significance of asking Moses to speak to the rock? Before we investigate this, look briefly at how Moses handles the grumblers of Israel.

> **So Moses took the rod from before the LORD, just as He commanded him.**
> **And Moses and Aaron gathered the assembly before the rock, and he said to them, "Listen now, you rebels; shall we bring you forth water for you out of this rock?"**
> **Then Moses lifted up his hand, and struck the rock twice with his rod: and water came forth abundantly, and the congregation and their beasts drank. (Numbers 20:9–11 NASB)**

Moses made two major errors here. The first is obvious. Rather than speaking to the rock as the LORD commanded him, he struck the rock like the first time, twice! Why twice?

There is also another significant difference between the first and second accounts of God providing water from the rock. The clue was given to us in **Numbers 20:10**. He called them "rebels." It's Moses's attitude. This time He was angry. Again! This time Moses was choosing to disobey God's direct instruction. In many of Moses's other sins, they were committed in ignorance of God's ways. God dealt with Moses gently and compassionately in these instances. However, this sin was a willful disobedience driven by anger. This is an anger that God had been patiently trying to heal Moses's heart from for the last forty years.

The second error is as follows. Moses said, "Shall we bring forth water for you?" It appears that Moses has begun to think that it's his and Aaron's own ability or righteousness that makes it possible to bring forth water, rather than humbly glorifying God alone. Pride! God picked up Moses as an angry, broken, and fearful murderer, with low self-esteem. He set him on a Rock and transformed his character into a strong, compassionate leader of the people of Israel. Now Moses, for this moment, while driven by anger, reverted back to his old thought patterns. He refused to allow God's healing work to be evident in his decision-making in this action. Moses began taking the credit for God's miracles. He forgot that God anointed and empowered him to do the miracles.

The truth is, it sounds like something all of us would do under the right conditions. Moses was at a weak moment. He was hurting over the loss of his sister. He was old and tired. He was tired of the desert and the whiny, sinful people. Satan is always watching us. He can sense when we are at our weakest point. So what is God to do with Moses?

> **But the LORD said unto Moses and Aaron, "Because you have not believed Me, to treat Me as Holy in the sight of the sons of Israel, therefore, you shall not bring this assembly into the land which I have given them." (Numbers 20:12 NASB)**

This seems kind of harsh, doesn't it? After all, Moses has been faithful to the LORD these forty years, and the LORD has worked through him to deliver the Israelites from persecution and captivity against great odds! And now, just as he is approaching the age of death, he would be kept from entering the promised land for making this one mistake! Let's look at the prophetic implications of this act of disobedience, and then maybe we can understand why the LORD disciplined Moses so severely.

Moses was asked to speak to the rock in the presence of all the people, and the water would gush forth. The first time, Christ (the Rock) was struck down (crucified) in order for the Holy Spirit (the water) to be poured out for any who would drink it (accept Christ as Savior). Water is life. Living water gushes out to sustain abundant life eternally. However, once atonement for the sin debt was paid by Christ's death on a cross, it was no longer necessary for Christ to be put to death a second time for our sin. All sins, past, present, and future, have already been atoned for. The death penalty has already been paid for believers. We don't have to earn it. Jesus doesn't have to keep dying over and over to pay it.

I remember the church camp days of my youth. The revival or camp preacher would ask at the end of the service if there was anyone who wanted to "rededicate his life to Christ." They would say, "Please come forward and pray with these deacons, elders, or myself down front! Or just lift your hand!" As if somehow the original dedication didn't work because your sin stuff kept happening. Their intentions were good; however, this is extremely bad theology! It somehow intertwines the subtle belief system that if we continue to sin, then our commitment must not have been sincere enough to save us, and we need to do it again, and again, and again. Wasn't Christ's death bloody enough to cover our degree of sin? It's one of Satan's greatest deceptions. Satan wants us to believe that God is sitting in heaven counting our sins.

Why didn't the preacher need to rededicate his life? Had they reached this level of perfect obedience that they no longer needed to "rededicate" their life? The underlying "false" belief is that we are saved when sinless perfection is attained based on our own ability to obey every law of the Word (and some added denominational rules outside the Word such as don't drink, don't dance, don't gamble, etc.). Again, man has lowered God's standard of righteousness way, way too low! It only takes one imperfect thought, emotional outburst, act of greed, selfishness, lie, etc., to sentence any human to death! Can anyone meet this standard? Ever? Christ, the ROCK, only had to be struck (crucified in a horrible, bloody death) ONE time to provide "living water" (His Holy Spirit in us) to give us eternal, regenerating life!

> **He who believes in Me, as the Scripture said, "From his innermost being will flow rivers of living water." (John 7:38)**

Remember the attributes of water? It is a protector, thermal blanket, detergent, solvent, and "flowing" medium to supply nutrients to grow life, while washing away waste toxins that destroy the living processes. The Holy Spirit is the "living" water that cleanses us from the old habitual belief patterns we became captive to while learning to cope in the fallen world system. The Holy Spirit's seal around us protects us from death and judgment (**2 Corinthians 1:22; Ephesians 1:2–13, 4:30**). The death penalty is forever paid in full! The Spirit of the living God has been fused into our being; and His regenerating, cleansing, nutrient-supplying truth (word, presence, and voice) is being put into work.

After the new birth in Christ has taken place, the Holy Spirit dwells in us. It is only necessary for us to speak to the Rock (Christ) to receive a gushing out of rivers of the Spirit's living power, enabling us to overcome (cleanse) habitual sins that still indwell our flesh, such as anger, immorality, selfishness, etc. When Moses struck the Rock a second time, it was as if he was saying that because of my emotion (anger), I am excused to deny the Spirit's power to change me, and I will rely on the old patterns of living I am acquainted with instead of submitting myself to God's new regenerated nature. This was a willful defiance of God's ways and comes with a heavy price, because God disciplines those He loves. He has a Father's responsibility to correct and perfect us until His work in us is finished (**Hebrews 12:4–11; Philippians 1:6**).

However, discipline is a continuous process just as a parent disciplines a child. Moses was asked to speak to the rock **"in the presence of the whole congregation."** He was to be a mentor to those less familiar with God's ways. This included Aaron as well as the Israelite people. God revealed himself to Moses so that Moses would reveal God and His ways to the people. The commission to us is the same today!

Moses's leadership was weakened from this point on. The consequences were twofold. The first was that He would not be allowed to enter the promised land, which represented a full, abundant life, while living on this earth. Moses's refusal to allow God to heal him completely from his anger issues prevented him from enjoying a full quality of life while on this earth. He died in a dry wilderness after struggling in it for forty years (if not one hundred twenty years). The second consequence was that his witness was damaged, which in turn did damage to Aaron and many others who would follow after Moses. Our choices harm others, even our loved ones. It is generational.

> **Then the Lord spoke to Moses and Aaron at Mount Hor by the border of the land of Edom, saying, "Aaron will be gathered to his people; for he shall not enter the land which I have given to the sons of Israel, because you rebelled against My command at the waters of Meribah.**
>
> **Take Aaron and his son Eleazar and bring them up to Mount Hor; and strip Aaron of his garments and put them on his son Eleazar. So Aaron will be gathered to his people, and will die there."**
>
> **So Moses did just as the Lord had commanded, and they went up to Mount Hor in the sight of all the congregation.**

> **After Moses had stripped Aaron of his garments and put them on his son Eleazar, Aaron died there on the mountain top. Then Moses and Eleazar came down from the mountain.**
>
> **When all the congregation saw that Aaron had died, all the house of Israel wept for Aaron thirty days. (Numbers 20:23–29 NASB)**

Moses had a tendency to act immediately without restraint over his emotions, causing him to sin. He later would approach God in prayer (speaking to the rock) to repent and seek the LORD's ways. In this particular event, God was trying to get Moses to speak to Him in prayer <u>before</u> acting out his emotions or false belief system. The LORD wanted to bring Moses's out-of-control emotions under control and reason truth in him. This would prevent a great deal of regrettable sin and harm. He was to do this in the presence of all the people, setting for them an example on how to please God as a people. Moses was to be a living light to the rest of the world (other nations, kingdoms, peoples).

Moses is in heaven and was truly chosen by God. However, his resistance to God's healing in this part of his life caused him to miss his blessing on earth. God's character here showed his firm discipline when the disobedience was willful. We as parents should follow this example and not give in to the child's whining. We should also be gentle and compassionate with our children when they commit sins out of ignorance. However, we should follow through with the teaching of why this sin is unacceptable, foretelling of its consequences. Remember to use God's Word as your source of truth and standard of right and wrong.

The other main point we should not forget is that to some people, we are the only reflection of God's character they may ever see. Our life is a living testimony. Our life is an animated love letter of God's love and plan for lost and dead souls around us. Some people become disenchanted with the idea of finding that love relationship with Christ because of what they see in other Christians.

Speak to the Rock, and Living Water will overflow and empower you to be an overcomer.

> **Be anxious for nothing, but in everything by prayer and supplication with thanksgiving let your requests be made known to God.**
> **And the peace of God which surpasses all comprehension, shall guard your hearts and your minds in Christ Jesus. (Philippians 4:6–7)**

Another question I wondered about for several years after I came to this initial understanding is why did God allow water to flow from the rock after Moses struck it in disobedience? Why didn't He just wait until Moses obeyed His proper instructions, to "speak to the rock" then allow water to flow? It seems God enabled more bad behavior and disobedience from Moses and other leaders who might have known what happened here.

My personal conclusion from everything I have learned about God is summed up in another one of God the Father's magnificent characteristics. GRACE! The people were hurting, thirsty, weary, and tired. God has compassion. He loves and cherishes the Israelite people. Israel is His chosen nation the world has their eye on. Christians (believers by faith) are his chosen children the world has their eye on. We make mistake after mistake. We commit sin after sin, yet He still supplies life, "living" water, which continues to flow to regenerate, to cleanse, and to quench our thirst. The rain falls on the just and the unjust.

Why did Moses strike twice? I think that we all can agree that he was angry. We usually don't stop striking after only one blow when we are angry either. In addition, the rock didn't gush forth water until the second blow. God paused and waited for Moses to catch himself. He didn't. Yet God in His compassion still gushed forth life-giving water.

They needed "flowing" water to drink and, for the ritual cleansing process from touching a corpse, to protect the people from disease. There's about to be a lot of corpses in the wilderness from the aging generation who would not trust God. That unbelieving generation would not enter the "promised land" because of their unbelief and disobedience to the precepts of God. These precepts were established for life from the beginning of creation.

God wasn't being a harsh, punishing Father here. The fact is life cannot grow in a world, people, or person riddled with rebellious sin. We are God's creation, and He is pure and holy. He can't live with sin and will not allow us to live in sin. It is contrary to His nature. God displayed compassion as He needed to remove the unbelieving generation fairly quickly so that He could bring the new generation of the Israelite nation into the "promised land" before they lost heart. Not allowing God's Spirit in us to overcome old habitual patterns of sin will cost us some degree of the abundant "promised land" life "flowing with milk and honey," while here on this earth!

The Holy Spirit still flows in us, convicting us toward confessing our sins and turning to Christ. It is never too late to turn your life around. Always remember that God is omniscient. He knows whether our intentions are pure and honest or whether we plan to continue to ignore His holiness. Asking someone to "rededicate their life to Christ" is incorrect theology that leaves a root of deception. There's no such thing. Either a person is already dedicated as His chosen with the indwelling Spirit in him, forever protected from death, or the person is not. A person not dedicated to God is still exposed to the full wrath of God and eternal death being outside of God's presence forever! There is no in-between measured by the degree of obedience or not. Don't cause a new or weak believer to "lose" heart! Keep reminding them of who they are "in Christ"! Stop trying to subtly convince them there are two classes of "Christians": the elite righteous and everyone else. It makes me puke, and the Scripture is very clear that it's a deception straight out of the pit of hell. Rather, let us encourage and build one another up. We are all the same, saved by His incredible GRACE!

# A "RIGHTEOUS" ANGER

THE TITLE OF THIS BOOK is "Is God Angry?" So, is He? When I have presented some of the events discussed in this book about Moses and God the Father's nature, especially when speaking about the killing of the 3,000, many people have a difficult time believing God didn't authorize Moses to act this out. Many also have a difficult time believing that God didn't "take" the life of the firstborn at the "Passover." Despite the avalanche of evidence presented in this book. Even with the many scriptures references throughout the entire bible presenting God the Father's nature as being gentle, patient, kind, compassionate, forgiving, etc… they still find it difficult. The very first words God proclaimed to Moses after Moses asked God to "show me Your ways" was in **Exodus 34:6–7.**

**Exodus 34:6–7**
**6 …."The LORD, the LORD God, compassionate and gracious, slow to anger, and abounding in lovingkindness and truth; who keeps lovingkindness for thousands, who forgives iniquity, transgression and sin; yet He will by no means leave *the guilty* unpunished, visiting the iniquity of the fathers on the children and on the grandchildren to the third and fourth generations."** (NASB)

Admittedly, these are some difficult passages that are often misunderstood as they relate to God the Father's character. But there is enough evidence to believe the truth presented here that God does hate sin, but is not angry with the person. When discussing the idea with others about God's character as not being angry with us, one of the most prominent (and usually the first) question commonly asked is "What about when Jesus was angry and overturned the moneychangers in the temple?" The natural follow-up questions would be, "Is there a "righteous anger? If so, what does it look like?"

Without the proper context, these misunderstood passages can cause a distorted view of God's character to appear as having an angry, harsh, and judgmental disposition. At the same time, a reader can easily overlook His gentleness, loving-kindness, patience, and compassion. This is not just an injustice to God the Father, but also harms our desire to seek relationship with Him and will affect the way we relate to our fellow man. I believe this statement says it most accurately, **"You will see yourself and treat others in the same way that you believe God treats and views you!"** The more I observe people, as they reveal their beliefs about the God as a father, the more I realize how true this is. For example: If a person believes God is angry at them, often they will easily become angered at others. They will usually have a problem with anger. They may also have a very low self-esteem.

If one believes God is quick to judge and punish without a patient, loving, gentle compassion, they will in turn become entrenched in legalism or perfectionism, judging and condemning others at every opportunity. This condemning belief system will make it very difficult to acknowledge or admit their own sin, because this would require self-condemnation. This type of person will attempt to justify their own wrong. Blaming others for almost everything, finding it very difficult to take responsibility for their own sins. I believe we saw these two examples in Moses life throughout the events researched in this book.

Another example Moses' life displayed was the belief that God is distant or didn't care about him. This belief system deeply affected his self-esteem. Low self-esteem is also a linked character trait in those who have experienced an absent father syndrome in a person's early childhood years. The father may have been present at home, but uninvolved in their life in various ways. Such as, seldom speaking to them, or acknowledging them, and almost never attending their activities (sports games, practices, plays, special events, etc...). A person with this "absent father syndrome" could develop a behavior pattern of being very withdrawn, finding it difficult to develop deep relationships. They may be very guarded, keeping themselves at a distance. They can become very sensitive to rejection, perceiving rejection in almost everything. They will usually have a constant need for reassurance of love and acceptance. They will have difficulty praying, as they feel that God doesn't hear or care about them. They can have great difficulty trusting God!

These are a few examples of how behavior is influenced by what we believe about God's nature and how He views us. As we saw in Moses' life, his beliefs about God's nature was shaped by his earthly father figure(s) of Pharaoh or the political leaders of the Egyptian culture. Even if Moses knew his natural father while in Egypt, how would the knowledge that his own father cast him out of the family protective unit into a river affect his view of God as a father?

In our own lives, if we were raised without a father, we would draw the father role model from other sources such as a coach, neighbor, TV, movies, or some other significant male father figure. Because of sin in the fallen creation, all of our role models of a father have been corrupted at least to some degree. This can be corrected over time by the power of the indwelling Spirit of God, and through a study of God the Father's true nature as revealed through the person of Jesus Christ, who is Jehovah God in the flesh (**John 1:1–2,14, 8:58**). It is this Spirit that provides the power to understand God's word, and strength to endure the healing process. In some cases, due to the extreme pain involved in unraveling the old father/child relationship, outside assistance of a trained counselor may be necessary.

Is there really something called "righteous" anger? I believe there is. But, does man know what it is? Probably not! The reason is that man develops his\her beliefs from what is programed into us by what we see and experience and how we process that information. Unfortunately, all men are raised in the fallen corrupt world. When we see anger displayed by others, we see a corrupt type of anger. Scripture tells us that **"the anger of man does not achieve the righteousness of God" (James 1:20)**. I believe this verse is telling us that when man expresses anger, most often sin is the result.

There is a righteous anger, but what does it look like? Anger can be a positive emotion if it moves us into action, and works to correct an injustice. Righteous anger is possible, but only to Spirit filled believers who learn to express it by the power of the Holy Spirit. Paul says in **Ephesians 4:27**, "Be angry but do not sin." The emphasis here may be more on alerting us toward caution when we feel the emotions of anger, rather than a command to "be angry." This verse is set in a chapter that details our identity being changed from a person who was deceived and held captive by sin, to a new identity in Christ. This new nature enables us by the power of the indwelling Spirit to overcome the old nature.

## Jesus and the Moneychangers

I believe Jesus gave us an example of righteous anger when he overturned the money changers in the temple, but this passage too, is often misunderstood. Some of you may have seen this event portrayed in movies or plays, but I doubt you would have imagined it as it really happened. Before I examine these scriptures in more detail, try to picture in your mind how Jesus behaved as He carried out these actions. These passages in **Matthew 21:12–22,** and **Luke 19:45–48** set the stage.

I have often seen and read of people who have used this event in Jesus' life as a justification for their own anger. I believe people who misunderstand passages like these, picture Jesus acting like someone else they have seen exhibit anger. Since man's anger is corrupt, and most often results in sin, how we visualized Him in this event, is most likely incorrect. So, a review of as much evidence as possible of this event is recommended if you truly desire to get a clear picture of what "righteous" anger might look like. Please, allow me to set the stage.

First, it's important to be aware that Jesus' cleansing the Temple occurred on two different occasions. Once in **John** chapter **2**, at the beginning of His ministry, and again 3 years later in **Mark 11:12–26 and Matthew 21:18–21**, near the end of His ministry. I want to give examples from both events, because the purpose of this book is to understand God the Father's nature as it applies to the display of a righteous anger. The main focus will be the event that takes place near the end of Jesus' ministry, just prior to His crucifixion. Both events took place during the Passover week. So, this latter event was the last week of Jesus' earthly life, which ended in His death.

I envision the bright sun shining on an abnormally busy day. People have come from all the surrounding regions to be here for this most celebrated "holy" day. There is a bustle of activity all around. Jesus comes riding into Jerusalem on a donkey. People recognize Him due to the buzzing news of all the miraculous events that have circulated throughout the regions. He has become a celebrity and the talk of every town. He has healed the blind, lame, sick, and diseased. He has shown compassion to the rejected and downtrodden. He displayed love and warm kindness toward the most egregious of that society, such as tax collectors, beggars, thieves, and those caught "in the very act of adultery!" He even raised people from the dead! The people recognize Him and immediately start shouting "Hosanna, Hosanna! Blessed be the name of the Lord!" They were paving the streets in front of Jesus with their coats, which was a sign of submission to the King and waiving palm branches, which was a Hebrew symbol of victory. They were glorifying Him as a military leader and King.

This is the day before the event of the temple cleansing was to take place. It's very likely the same day described in **Mark 11:12–26**

**and Matthew 21:18–21**. Strategically placed in scripture, is a conversation with the disciples about this fig tree that was not producing fruit. Jesus, on His way into Jerusalem and to the temple for Passover, passed a fig tree, which was in bloom, but not producing fruit. Jesus cursed the tree. The next morning, on their way back out of Jerusalem, after overturning the moneychangers in the Temple, Jesus and His disciples passed this same fig tree, which He had cursed earlier. It was withered from the roots up. Is this just a side event, or a significant reason why the money changers event was placed right in the middle of this fig tree account? I believe they are connected.

In **Matthew 23:37,** Matthew described Jesus stopping at the top of the Mount of Olives and weeping over Jerusalem, saying, "Jerusalem, Jerusalem, who kills the prophets and stones those who are sent to her! How often I wanted to gather your children together, the way a hen gathers her chicks under her wings, and you were unwilling." Jesus had longed to bring them into an eternal peace, providing protection over them and ensure their life. However, they had not recognized who He truly was, and what His purpose was. Again, this was just prior to the moneychangers being cast out of the Temple.

The fig tree event was a foreshadowing of this overturning of the money changers event. The non-productive fig tree represented the religious system of that day, which did not produce any righteous fruit. Therefore, Jesus condemned it and the fig tree withered and died overnight. So too, Jesus condemned this Jewish hierarchy of traditional ritualistic religion that produced no fruit (righteousness). After this cleansing of the temple, Jesus pointed out the Pharisees' hypocrisy in the "seven woes (**Matthew 23**)." During this confrontation, He said, "They tie up heavy burdens and lay them on men's shoulders, but they themselves are unwilling to move them with so much as a finger (**Matthew 23:4**)." He also said, "You travel about on sea and land to make one proselyte, and when he becomes one, you make him twice as much a son of hell as yourselves (**Matthew 23:15**)." His inference was about heaping a load of "laws" that no man could fully keep. Not even themselves. The Pharisees enjoyed condemning them and imposing expensive religious ordinances that lined their pockets, to atone for their law breaking.

Jesus was on a mission that day, to condemn and curse the religious system that produced no fruit! Within approximately 40-years the Temple and all of Jerusalem would be destroyed, and the non-producing religious system would be withered from the roots up, never to exist again.

Now I want to examine the featured event as it really happened. Jesus, in the process of this eviction, told them they had turned His

"House of Prayer" into a robber's den! This is best made clear in the gospel of **Mark 11:15–17.**

**Mark 11:15–17**
**15 On reaching Jerusalem, Jesus entered the temple area and began driving out those who were buying and selling there. He overturned the tables of the money changers and the benches of those selling doves,**
**16 and would not allow anyone to carry merchandise through the temple courts.**
**17 And as he taught them, he said, "Is it not written: "My house will be called a house of prayer for all nations'? But you have made it 'a den of robbers." (NIV)**

Note two things about this passage. First, notice the money-changers were buying and selling, not just selling. Why were they buying, at this annual Passover, if their purpose was to sell to those who needed a sacrifice, to atone for their sin? It is a known historical fact that the merchants had a practice of sitting at the temple, buying goods at wholesale, and selling them to the public at retail, therefore making a profit.

What's wrong with making a profit? Nothing, except in this case, they were making a profit from an illness that no man could cure, sin! This illness resulted in certain eternal death, and these merchants were minimizing the real significance of this plight to a mere casual event of everyday life. To them, it was no big deal, even though God instituted this sacrificial ordinance earlier so that this nation could live in the presence of a pure and holy God!

Second, notice in this passage the animal of sacrifice mentioned was a dove. While other passages tell us that sheep and oxen were also being sold there, Mark draws attention to the merchants here who were selling doves. **Leviticus 12:8 and 14:21–22** provides more detailed information about this issue.

**Leviticus 12:8**
**8 If she cannot afford a lamb, she is to bring two doves or two
young pigeons (*doves*), one for a burnt offering and the other for
a sin offering. In this way the priest will make atonement for her,
and she will be clean.'" (NIV)**

Doves were the designated sacrifice for the poor. Not only were
these merchants making a mockery of God's ordinance for covering
man's sin, but they were also taking advantage of the most oppressed
people of the land, all in the name of holy religion, of course! The
widow, or the prostitute, or the thief, the poor hard working construction worker or farm hand. Many had travelled a long distance
for this annual event. They came with a heart's desire to feel clean
before the Almighty God, who has the power to change their position in life. Give them acceptance, forgiveness and a hope for the
future. These folks would financially have the least to spare to be
able to purchase this sacrifice to make atonement for their sin. Yet
they were required to pay the elevated price for that right standing
according to the religious ritual of that day!

Jesus had been watching this injustice all His life. It was now,
less than one week before His own ultimate sacrificial death, He
chose to correct this wrong …., again! Jesus would not allow these
merchants to even pass through the temple with their goods. How
was He able to command this kind of authority? The chief priests
and scribes wondered this same thing (**Matthew 21:23–27, Mark
11:27–33**), which I will address later.

As mentioned earlier, when Jesus entered the Temple, all the
merchants were <u>sitting</u> in their respective seats. It's possible that these
seats were occupied by the same merchants year after year. I imagine
that the designated spots, closest to the main thoroughfares, is for
the merchants with the longest tenure or the greatest political clout.
How would Jesus get these callous hard-hearted robbers out of the
temple? If He simply asked them, they would probably laugh and
want to know by whose authority. It wouldn't be "Christlike" to turn

over their seats with the merchants still sitting in them. Was there another way? I picture Jesus, in His infinite wisdom, first gently turning over their table of money. This most likely got the merchants out of their seats. With money being their god, they would have instantly stood up! While standing, He turned over their chairs as they stood in disbelief.

What about the whip? This shows us Jesus' great patience, just like the patience He had as He watched this injustice all of His life before taking action at just the right time. The account in **John 2:13–17** tells us that He made a scourge of cords and drove them out. I don't know how long it takes to make a whip out of cords, but one thing is for sure, He did not come in there just because He was having a bad hair day and fly off the handle in an uncontrollable burst of rage. That morning, He probably sat on the temple steps watching it all unfold for a couple of hours, while He made the whip. This brings us to the next question, "Did he whip the moneychangers?" Examine the passage in John carefully.

**John 2:1516**
**15 And He made a scourge of cords, and drove *them* all out of the temple, with the sheep, and the oxen; and He poured out the coins of the money changers, and overturned their tables;**
**16 and to those who were selling the doves He said, "Take these things away; stop making My Father's house a place of business."**
(NASB)

The order was "... drove them all out of the temple, <u>with the sheep, and the oxen</u>." This passage indicates that He probably cracked the whip and the sound started the livestock stampeding. I don't think any of them wanted to attempt to wrestle a strong man with a whip to the ground, besides they didn't know where His authority might have come from. Surely no man would be bold enough to carry on like this in such a "holy place" unless he had special authority to do so. The Israelite religious leaders were still under the authority of the Roman occupation, and under their system of law. Even Roman guards were in authority over the Priests (Pharisees Scribes, and Sadducees). And Pilate was in town, something was up. Had they opposed Jesus and later found out that He had special granted authority to do such, they would have most likely found themselves in deep trouble or even dead. The guilt of their own sin may also have had something to do with their lack of retaliation. In addition, the common people of all Israel loved Him, they flocked to Him. Opposing Him publicly might have caused a civil riot.

In the re-enactments I have seen of this event in movies and plays, Jesus is depicted as wildly and angrily picking up and throwing the money changer's tables and money. Even pushing the people out of His way. Is this really the way He acted? What's written gives insight to determine if this is the real story or not. The word for "cast out" or "drove out" is the same word used in all 4-Gospels. The Greek word is "***ekballo***," it means *to eject, expel, put out, send away*. The root words indicate this action as being done in a deliberate, orderly manner. There are other words in the Greek language for violent forcing out of a people or things, which are **not** used here in any of the 4-gospel accounts.

The other word we should examine is the one for "overturned" or "overthrew." This word in the account of John is "***anastrepho***," which means to overturn. It's from the root word, which means "to <u>behave self</u>, <u>have conversation</u>, overthrow." Examination of these words indicate that Jesus quietly, with a groaning, inaudible, mumbling under his breath (whisper), deliberately, and gently turned over

the tables, poured out their money (as opposed to throwing or fling-
ing it) and cracked the whip to move the animals out, speaking to
them as He commanded with authority without raising His voice.

This type of behavior makes more sense as you look at the
chief priests and the scribe's reaction. They wanted to know who
gave Him the authority to do these things as His behavior indicated
He had a superior authority to theirs to act (**Mark 11: 27–28**). If
Jesus was running around in an angry rage, His behavior would have
been so suspect that He would have been considered a madman to
be restrained, even by the Roman guards. They were employed to
keep the peace and provide order and protection from civil unrest.
Instead, His quiet, deliberate, and gentle manner, acting with commanding authority, made the onlookers (especially the priests and
scribes) wonder if He possibly had authority from someone superior
to their authority. This prompted them to ask, "By what authority
are you doing these things, and who gave you this authority?" His
authority was from The Only Creator of the Universe. The "I AM!"

## Matthew 21:14–15
**14 And *the* blind and *the* lame came to Him in the temple, and
He healed them.**
**15 But when the chief priests and scribes saw the wonderful
things that He had done, and the children who were shouting in
the temple, "Hosanna to the Son of David," they were indignant,**
(NASB)

There's one more bit of evidence in Matthew's account (**Matthew
21:12–17**). Notice especially (**verses 14** and **15**). The blind and the
lame came to him to be healed immediately following this event. The
children also were coming to Him in praise and worship immediately
following this event. The Greek word for children is "pais," which
describes slave or servant children. Do you think a slave or servant
child who may have possibly felt or witnessed the sting of a whip
would have run to Jesus in worship and praise if He would have acted
in a violent, out of control anger cracking a whip? I don't think so.

Did He raise His voice? As a believer, we are required to put our full trust (confidence in) Christ. In **John 1:1** he says that Christ <u>is</u> the Word. **Isaiah 42:2** tells us when prophesying of Christ that **"He will not cry out or raise** *His voice***, Nor make His voice heard in the street."** If all prophesy of scripture is absolutely true, and I believe it is, then Jesus did not yell, but rather had a quiet demeanor.

Jesus also stayed the rest of the day teaching in the temple until evening. Not the actions of a man who feared being arrested for violence. In **Mark 11:18–19, John 2:47–48** Jesus waited patiently to correct a terrible injustice being done to the poor and oppressed. These poor and oppressed people had a sincere desire to make atonement to God for their sin, in accordance with God's provision. His actions were not only aimed at granting justice and compassion towards the poor and oppressed, but also toward the Scribes, Priests, and Pharisees, in an attempt to awaken them to the truth, and an awareness of their corrupt and fruitless religion. He hoped to save some of them from their own blindness. In **Acts 6:7**, it does indicate that some of those priests did eventually commit their lives to Him.

Is God Angry? The answer is yes, but with sin, not with man. And His anger looks very, very, different than man's anger. As you review all of the accounts of this event, you may notice that the word anger is never used in describing what Jesus did. The word that was mentioned is "zeal," which is a fervent, jealous indignation. From a root word meaning "heat or hot, to boil." Heating to a boiling point is a process of purifying corruptive harmful impurities from water. Jesus felt the emotion of anger, but never allowed it to control Him, thus causing sin. Jesus loves all mankind, both those guilty of the corrupt religious system and the oppressed common class who wanted to have atonement for sin. Not that I have by any means mastered it, but I want to learn to act in this kind of self-controlled authority. Picturing Jesus in action as given by scripture with the description pointed out in this chapter, helps provide proper perspective to enable believers to model this type of "righteous anger."

How does this perspective reflect on the many religious systems in our world today? There is only one that will produce fruit. What is fruit? Fruit is a changed heart, from one that is self-centered to one that displays the self-sacrificing, life-saving love of God the Father's character. Churches, as a whole, often can put too much focus on programs and projects rather than on loving the people around them. Appearance has become paramount.

Please become mindful of the "Pharisees" disease. Exercise caution not to fall into the trap Jesus referred to when he said "They tie up heavy burdens and lay them on men's shoulders, but they themselves are unwilling to move them with so much as a finger." This is done by imposing a strict legalistic standard of laws that determine your "acceptance" as a person into their church community. Not that "lawlessness" should be permitted, but basing a person's acceptance on their ability to perform some pre-established list of "do's" and "don'ts" will only cause people to run away from the body of believers and toward wherever they can find acceptance, usually the lowest common denominator. Jesus didn't do this, and neither should we. Legalism kills, grace saves. Not a single one of us can carry out the Ten Commandments without a flaw. So, we should all come alongside each other, loving and accepting each other and allow the Holy Spirit to do the convicting and disciplining work in the person next to us, as well as in ourselves.

Churches are made up of believers given free will to choose life and truth, or reject it for some lie or deception. Our life, if we are to bear fruit, should be committed toward knowing and obeying the truth, not forcibly imposing it on others. If they are a believer, they will follow Christ, that's why we're called "followers." If they're not, the Holy Spirit's convicting work will kill them inside with kindness and they will either fall in love with Him or reject Him and leave the church. We should love and accept every person in our sphere of influence. Don't condemn them or ourselves when sin happens. It will. The Holy Spirit will deal with each person's sin as they are able to bear it. Be available to share the truth when they are ready to receive it. Speak to them with gentleness and love, looking at your own still flawed condition. If they find safety and acceptance in your relationship to them, see Godly character in your life's choices, and honesty when you admit your own failures, then they will confide in you when the pain is severe enough. Always be ready to give your testimony to everyone who asks you about the hope that is in you. Always let love rule the day.

Even in anger, Jesus acted with gentleness, compassion, and self-control. In this anger He was still reaching out to all of mankind in order to provide a way of salvation. This is an example of righteous anger. I would guess it to be different than the previous image you had before. I know it was for me. As I study and know man, I find more flaws and unhealed sin. As I study and know Christ, I find more sinless perfection and loving compassion. Keep your eyes on Him instead of your teacher, pastor, christian friend, parent, etc...

# Endnotes

[1]  J. Warner Wallace, *Cold-Case Christianity: A Homicide Detective Investigates the Claims of the Gospels.*

**Jews** *believe Jesus was Mary's son, was a teacher* (rabbi), had many disciples, was respected, performed miracles, claimed to be the Messiah, and was crucified on the cross. They also acknowledge His followers reported Jesus was raised from the dead.

**Muslims** *believe Jesus was born of a virgin, is to be revered and respected, was a prophet,* was a wise teacher who worked miracles, ascended to heaven, and will come again.

**Ahmadiyya Muslims** *believe Jesus may have been born of a virgin, was a prophet and wise teacher, worked miracles, and was crucified on a cross.*

**Baha'i** *believe Jesus came from God, was a wise teacher who had a divine and human nature, worked miracles, and was crucified and resurrected as an atonement for humanity.*

**Hindus** *believe Jesus was a holy man,* was a wise teacher, and is a "god."

**Buddhists** *believe Jesus was an enlightened man and a wise teacher.*

**New Age** *believers maintain Jesus was a wise moral teacher.*

[2]  Ibid.

[3]  Bharath Ramsundar, "The Ferocious Complexity of the Cell," June 3, 2016.

[4]  European Molecular Biology Laboratory, "Impact of Genome Reduction on Bacterial Metabolism and Its Regulation," *Science* (2009). DOI 10.1126/science.1177263.

[5]  Wikipedia, as of April 2019.

# ABOUT THE AUTHOR

I WAS BORN IN DALLAS, Texas, and raised in a Southern Baptist home. My father was a pastor throughout my lifetime. I became the prodigal son at an early age, having engaged in socially dysfunctional behavior patterns such as drug use, jail time due to crime, lifestyle exposure to vices related to the rock music industry as a musician, sexual addiction, etc. For years as a believer, I led a double life of ministry in the church while secretly struggling with addictions I couldn't control. The ensuing damage of those lifestyle choices led to multiple marriage failures and difficulty trusting relationships. Possessing a type A–driven personality, I succeeded at most endeavors, including business ownerships. However, I had a deep-seated anger that was destroying me from the inside. In a quest to find healing, through counseling and research of the Scripture, God led me to the one thing that is able to change the course of my life: an understanding of who God is as a "father."